LUTON SIXTH FORM COLLEGE

WITHDRAWN

26. OCT 1972	15. OCT 1982	
15. MAY 1973	31. OCT 1985	
25 FEB 1974	12. DEC. 1985	
18. JUN 1974	- 7. JAN 1986	
16. MAR. 1976	- 2. NOV 1988	
21. OCT 1976		
- 2. MAR. 1978	21. JAN 1997	
13. NOV 1978	2 0 MAR 2002	
- 2. DEC. 1980	1 1 MAR 2014	
12. JAN 1981		
13. OCT 1981	1 7 MAR 2014	
15. OCT 1982		

Literature in Perspective

Shakespeare

Kenneth H. Grose and B. T. Oxley

Evans Brothers Limited, London

Published by Evans Brothers Limited
Montague House, Russell Square, London, W.C.1
© Kenneth H. Grose & B. T. Oxley 1965
First published 1965
Reprinted 1969

Set in 11 on 12pt. Fournier and printed in Great Britain by
C. Tinling & Co. Ltd., Liverpool, London and Prescot

237   44409   7 cased   PR 4918
237   44539   5 limp

Literature in Perspective

Of recent years, the ordinary man who reads for pleasure has been gradually excluded from that great debate in which every intelligent reader of the classics takes part. There are two reasons for this: first, so much criticism floods from the world's presses that no one but a scholar living entirely among books can hope to read it all; and second, the critics and analysts, mostly academics, use a language that only their fellows in the same discipline can understand.

Consequently criticism, which should be as 'inevitable as breathing'—an activity for which we are all qualified—has become the private field of a few warring factions who shout their unintelligible battle cries to each other but make little communication to the common man.

Literature in Perspective aims at giving a straightforward account of literature and of writers—straightforward both in content and in language. Critical jargon is as far as possible avoided; any terms that must be used are explained simply; and the constant preoccupation of the authors of the Series is to be lucid.

It is our hope that each book will be easily understood, that it will adequately describe its subject without pretentiousness, so that the intelligent reader who wants to know about Donne or Keats or Shakespeare will find enough in it to bring him up to date on critical estimates.

Even those who are well read, we believe, can benefit from a lucid exposition of what they may have taken for granted, and perhaps—dare it be said?—not fully understood.

K. H. G.

Shakespeare

The present writers, of different generations and differing in their approaches to Shakespeare, are teachers and not scholars; we lay no claim to original ideas. We have tried in a short book to give an account of Shakespeare's plays, and the conditions in which they were created, in the light of as much modern scholarship as we have been able to read. More than any other writer, the acknowledged master of them all is in danger of being swamped by the enormous mass of critical opinion that surrounds him.

We have tried to assess the most important of this in several fields of study and to present a coherent and comprehensive picture: to put Shakespeare into perspective.

Because we have not tried to write a scholarly book, we have not used the word 'probably' in every sentence that, strictly speaking, needs it. This means that we have sometimes stated as a fact something which has not been fully established.

The reading lists have been kept realistically short. The books recommended here are indispensable and among the more intelligible; and nearly all of them are readily available, many of them as paperbacks (indicated by PB). References in the text are to Peter Alexander's *Tudor Edition* of the complete works (Collins, 1951). The drawings are by Anthony Holbrook.

K. H. G.

B. T. O.

Contents

The Authors

Kenneth H. Grose, M.A., is the Senior English Master at
Bradford Grammar School.
B. T. Oxley, M.A., Ph.D., is Lecturer in English at the
University of Bradford.

Acknowledgements

Picasso's *Guernica* © S.P.A.D.E.M., Paris, 1965, is reproduced from the Pallas Gallery Print. The facsimile of Shakespeare's handwriting and the pages from the First and Second Quartos are reproduced by permission of the Trustees of the British Museum.

I

Life, Works and Times

Shakespeare's life, the type of society in which he lived, the culture of Renaissance England, the nature of English drama in the decades before he started writing, and the political history of the period: all these things are factors in the making of his plays; perhaps the most important factor—the philosophical ideas of what is known as 'The Elizabethan World Picture'—is treated separately in Chapter 6.

SHAKESPEARE'S LIFE AND WORK

If you find it helpful to arrange facts in patterns, you may see Shakespeare's life in three phases: (a) from 1564 to about 1590; (b) from about 1590 to about 1610; (c) from about 1610 to 1616. The middle phase, which represents the twenty-odd years of his working life, could be sub-divided—purely for convenience—at 1603, into Elizabethan and Jacobean (although 'Elizabethan' is often loosely used to describe a much longer period than that of the actual reign).

When Shakespeare was born, Elizabeth had been queen for six years. Stratford was a midlands market-town of probably fewer than one thousand people, in a relatively undeveloped land of three millions, nearly ninety per cent of whom were country born and bred. London, already a major European town, was about ninety miles away.

Shakespeare's father came into Stratford from a neighbouring farm in the 1550's, set up in various trades, prospered, bought property, and married. By the time William, his first son and third child, was four, Shakespeare senior had worked through a succession of local government offices to become the town's leading citizen. In 1576 he applied for a gentleman's coat of arms, but after this time seems to have been less successful and withdrew from public life.

Presumably the young Shakespeare, after attending what was known as a 'petty-school', went to the local grammar school (free for him, and only half a mile from his home) from roughly 1570 to 1580. Here he would study little but Latin, mastering its grammar, and getting a taste of its literature. He would read, at least in part, authors like Terence, Virgil, Horace, Plautus, Cicero, Caesar, Sallust, Juvenal, Martial, Livy and Ovid (there still exists a copy of *Metamorphoses* with his signature). He may also have studied rhetoric—the art of spoken discourse, which played such a large part in Renaissance education. Whatever the details of his education were, Shakespeare was playing with both written and spoken language for something like eight or nine hours a day, six days a week, while he was at school.

In 1582, aged eighteen, he married a woman eight years older than himself, and their first child was born six months later. We do not know how he earned his living after leaving school; we do not even know where he was. It seems likely that by 1590 (taking this date simply as a round number) he was in London, establishing himself in the theatre, perhaps as a member of one of the companies he had watched while it was on tour and playing in his home town. (Between 1569 and 1587 there were twenty-five visits to Stratford by ten or more companies. For at least one of those years Shakespeare's father, as bailiff, would have had to license the players and attend their opening performance. In 1587 itself no fewer than five companies played in the town.)

By 1590, then, Shakespeare may have been a member of an acting company; he may also have been one of a literary circle patronised by the Earl of Southampton. In 1592 he seems to be referred to in a contemporary pamphlet as a rising dramatist; by 1595, perhaps helped with a gift from Southampton, he was a sharer in the recently formed acting company with which he was to remain for the rest of his working life (see Chapter 2), and was sufficiently important to be named as one of the men who, on the company's behalf, received payment for court performances; in 1597 he had made enough money to buy New Place, one of the best houses in Stratford, where he made further investments later; in 1599 he invested in the company's new theatre.

How he spent his time between 1590 and 1603 is not known in any detail. Presumably he was mostly in London, occupied with the running of a repertory theatre; perhaps he revised old plays; he certainly wrote new ones. It has been suggested that during the summer months of plague infection, when his colleagues went on tour, he returned to Stratford to do the writing which was his greatest contribution to the financial success of the company.

During these thirteen years Shakespeare wrote something like twenty-six plays (plus the two narrative poems *Venus and Adonis* and *The Rape of Lucrece*—published in 1593 and 1594— and perhaps the *Sonnets*—published in 1609). This represents well over half his complete work, and brings him to the verge of his greatest achievements. In the following lists the dates of composition can only be approximate, and you must not take the detailed order of the plays too seriously. The general pattern of what is known as 'the Shakespeare Canon' is now fairly well-established, but scholars still argue over the details. In any case we do not know how much Shakespeare may have revised his plays. Some textual-critics, for example J. Dover Wilson, believe that they can distinguish different 'strata' of verse within one play: thus, Wilson argues that in *A Midsummer Night's Dream* the lovers' dialogue with the love-plot was written in 1592 or before, the rustics and fairies were added in the winter of 1594, and the whole revised for Southampton's wedding in 1598. The date in brackets is that of the first publication; for an explanation of Folios (F) and Quartos (Q) see Chapter 3.

1590-91	1 *Henry the Sixth*	(F 1623)
	2 *Henry the Sixth*	(Q 1594)
	3 *Henry the Sixth*	(Q 1595)
1592	*Richard the Third*	(Q 1597)
	Titus Andronicus	(Q 1594)

1593	*The Comedy of Errors*	(F 1623)
	The Taming of the Shrew	(F 1623)
1594	*The Two Gentlemen of Verona*	(F 1623)
	Love's Labour's Lost	(Q 1598)
1595	*Romeo and Juliet*	(Q 1597)
	Richard the Second	(Q 1597)
1596	*A Midsummer Night's Dream*	(Q 1600)
	King John	(F 1623)
1597	*The Merchant of Venice*	(Q 1600)
	1 Henry the Fourth	(Q 1598)
1598	*2 Henry the Fourth*	(Q 1600)
	The Merry Wives of Windsor	(Q 1602)
1599	*Henry the Fifth*	(Q 1600)
	Much Ado about Nothing	(Q 1600)
	Julius Caesar	(F 1623)
1600	*As You Like It*	(F 1623)
	Twelfth Night	(F 1623)
1601	*Hamlet*	(Q 1603)
1602	*Troilus and Cressida*	(Q 1609)
1603	*All's Well that Ends Well*	(F 1623)
	Measure for Measure	(F 1623)

After 1603 Shakespeare came to the top of his profession. Legally one of King James's personal servants, he was awarded material as special livery for the coronation procession, and it was his company, often performing his own plays, that was most frequently called upon for court-performances. He was also at the height of his imaginative powers. Again, the detail of his life is not known, but the pattern was presumably similar to that of the earlier years, except that he seems to have relinquished acting. When the company obtained a second theatre in 1608, Shakespeare again invested, but he seems to have retired from an active part in the group after 1610 (to use another round number). By 1613 he was settled at New Place, the house he had bought sixteen years earlier; perhaps there were occasional visits to London, but it was in Stratford that he died in 1616.

How much Shakespeare earned as a professional and popular

writer is difficult to determine. His income presumably would fluctuate with that of the company, and it is unlikely that he ever made much more than £200 a year (Elizabethan values have to be multiplied by about fifteen to get a very rough modern equivalent). This was certainly enough to allow him to live very comfortably, and all the evidence seems to suggest that he knew how to look after himself very well financially, and that he became far more prosperous than most of the other writers of his time.

During this last period he wrote:

1604	*Othello*	(Q 1622)
1605	*Timon of Athens*	(F 1623)
1606	*King Lear*	(Q 1608)
	Macbeth	(F 1623)
1607	*Antony and Cleopatra*	(F 1623)
	Coriolanus	(F 1623)
1609	*Cymbeline*	(F 1623)
1610	*The Winter's Tale*	(F 1623)
1611	*The Tempest*	(F 1623)
1612	*Henry the Eighth*	(F 1623)

Here are ten plays written in about nine years, and with the twenty-six already listed, they make up the whole canon—technically all the plays printed in the First Folio of 1623. Most modern critics would add *Pericles*, written about 1608 (Q 1609), but how much of this play, and of *Henry the Eighth*, is by Shakespeare is not known. These are the thirty-seven plays of most collected editions, which may also include parts of what is known as 'the Shakespeare Apocrypha' of plays attributed either wholly or in part to him. The most famous of these are a lost play called *Cardenio*, *The Two Noble Kinsmen* and *Sir Thomas More* (the MS of this last still exists; some think that part of it is in Shakespeare's handwriting—see the facsimile facing p. 72).

ENGLISH RENAISSANCE CULTURE

When modern sociologists discuss 'culture' in the sense of art and entertainment, they distinguish 'high' or 'élite' culture from 'popular'. Nowadays these things are fairly distinct: the people who listen to pop-singers are not on the whole the people who attend concerts of chamber music; readers of the kind of books discussed in Richard Hoggart's *The Uses of Literacy* are not usually readers of literature with a capital 'L'; buyers of rude comic postcards at the seaside do not usually visit art-galleries. In some ways the distinction applied in Shakespeare's time. Much of the culture to be discussed in the following pages was clearly produced by an élite for the enjoyment of an élite; it is interesting that when Marlowe's play *Tamburlaine the Great* was printed, the comic scenes which had appeared when the play was performed on the popular stage were excluded, on the grounds that they were 'far unmeet for the matter . . . though (haply) they have been, of some vain, conceited fondlings, greatly gaped at, what times they were showed upon the stage in their graced deformities'.

One of the most interesting things about Shakespeare's work is the way in which it is astride both cultures. He experienced the high art of his time, getting from it ideas as well as material for stories; but he worked in a popular entertainment industry, writing plays which have their roots in the native dramatic tradition. The simplest way of putting this is to say that a play of his could be seen and enjoyed by the penny-paying ground-lings at The Globe, where the audience in any case covered a much wider social range than in a modern theatre, as well as by the courtiers in the royal palaces.

The major feature of the English Renaissance was that it was a book culture, transmitted through printed texts and not through manuscripts. Caxton had set up his Westminster press less than a hundred years before Shakespeare's birth, and the Bodleian Library was opened in 1602. While Shakespeare was not an intellectual like John Donne, or a classicist like Ben Jonson, there is plenty of evidence—for example, the wide range of source-material he used—that he was a well-read man. His grammar-school education would make him a sound enough Latinist; he could probably manage Italian and French. And, of course, you can pick up a knowledge of books from conversation—particularly if, like Shakespeare, you live in the literary world. (Shakespeare's likely reading is set out in the introduction and summary to K. Muir's *Shakespeare's Sources*, Vol. I, Methuen, 1957.)

By 1590 the great figures of the early English Renaissance were long dead: More, Erasmus, Coverdale, Wyatt, Surrey, Ascham, Elyot. But the impetus of intellectual excitement continued. These are some of the major books published in the decades preceding Shakespeare's arrival in London (we have concentrated upon those most likely to have been read by Shakespeare; we quote from several of them in Chapter 6; the dates are those of the first editions only—in several cases there are later, much enlarged ones).

GENERAL

1547   *A Book of Homilies.*
1553   Wilson's *Art of Rhetoric.*
1559   *Mirror for Magistrates.*
1561   Hoby's translation of *The Courtier.*
1563   Foxe's *The Acts and Monuments of the Church* —better known as *The Book of Martyrs.*
1568   *The Bishops' Bible.*
1570   Ascham's *The Schoolmaster.*
1577   Holinshed's *The Chronicles of England, Scotland and Ireland*—the immediate source of the history plays, with Hall's *The Union of the Noble and Illustrious Families of York and Lancaster* (1542).
1579   North's translation of Plutarch's *Lives.* . . . —the immediate source of the Roman plays.
1586   Translation of de la Primaudaye's *The French Academy.*
1589   Hakluyt's *Principal Navigations.* . . .

POETRY AND FICTION

1565   Golding's translation of Ovid's *Metamorphoses* (Bks. 1-4).

1566 Painter's *The Palace of Pleasure*—a collection of short stories which supplied Shakespeare with some of his plots.

1576 *A Paradise of Dainty Devices*—one of the most popular poetical miscellanies.

1578 Lyly's *Euphues*—a romance written in an extremely affected and very influential style.

1579 Spenser's *The Shepherd's Calendar*—usually regarded as the first major achievement of Elizabethan literature.

1588 Greene's *Pandosto*—a romance which is the source of *The Winter's Tale*.

In 1590, of the thinkers and non-dramatic writers usually associated with this period, Spenser, Raleigh, Lodge, Hakluyt, Fulke-Greville and Hooker were in their thirties (as Sidney would have been had he survived the Battle of Zutphen in 1586); Bacon, Daniel and Drayton were about Shakespeare's own age; Nashe was twenty, Donne in his late teens and Robert Burton was a schoolboy. During Shakespeare's working life the following books were published:

GENERAL

1594 Hooker's *Of the Laws of Ecclesiastical Polity*.
1595 Sidney's *Apology for Poetry*.
1597 Bacon's *Essays*.
1603 Florio's translation of Montaigne's *Essays*.
    Holland's translation of Plutarch's *Morals*.
1605 Bacon's *Advancement of Learning*.
1611 Authorised Version of The Bible.

POETRY AND FICTION

1590 Spenser's *Fairy Queen*—completed in 1596; this is one of the central books of the period.
    Sidney's *Arcadia*—a romance from which Shakespeare obtained the *King Lear* sub-plot.
    Lodge's *Rosalind*—a romance; the source for *As You Like It*.

1591	Greene's *Cony Catching*—first of a series on Elizabethan confidence-tricksters.
	Sidney's *Astrophel and Stella*—a sonnet-sequence written *c.* 1580.
1592	Nashe's *Pierce Penniless*—containing the first reference to Shakespeare's work.
1595	Daniel's *History of the Civil Wars*—a narrative poem covering the same ground as Shakespeare's histories.
1598	Chapman's translation of part of *The Iliad.*
	Marlowe's *Hero and Leander.*
1600	*England's Helicon*—one of the best Elizabethan anthologies of lyrical poetry.
1611	Donne's *Anatomy of the World*—Donne's poems were circulated in manuscript in the '90's.
1612	Drayton's *Polyolbion*—a topographical poem.

Of these writers Greene, Nashe, Spenser, Marlowe and Hooker died before Shakespeare. Hakluyt, Raleigh and Daniel were dead by 1620; Lodge, Bacon, Florio and Fulke-Greville by 1630; Drayton, Donne and Chapman by 1640. In 1616 the figures we associate with Commonwealth and Restoration England were appearing: Hobbes, Herrick, Herbert and Walton were in their twenties; Sir Thomas Browne, Waller and Oliver Cromwell in their teens; Fuller, Milton, Clarendon, Jeremy Taylor and Crashaw were all children. Marvell was born in 1621, Bunyan in 1628, Dryden in 1631 and Locke in 1632—sixty-eight years after the birth of the man with whom we are concerned.

It must not be thought that books, however important they were, represented the whole of Renaissance culture. There was the architecture of the great Elizabethan houses like Longleat, Hardwick New Hall, Wollaton, Losely. There was the painting —admittedly not of the highest importance by European standards—of the miniaturists Nicholas Hilliard (who was fifty-three in 1590) and Isaac Oliver (who was about the same age as Shakespeare). There was, above all, music.

This—particularly from about 1600 to 1615—was one of the greatest periods of English music, especially as far as

B

sacred music, the air and the madrigal were concerned. Musical training was considered part of the education of a civilised man; philosophically (see Chapter 6) music was regarded as one of the symbolical keystones of the divine order of things. There was a large group of English composers: in 1590 Thomas Tallis was only five years dead; Byrd was in his forties; Rosseter and Morley (who may have written some of the original settings for Shakespeare's lyrics) were in their thirties; Dowland, Bull, Campion, Farnaby were in their twenties; Weelkes and Willbye were in their teens, and Orlando Gibbons was a child. Morley's *Canzonets to Three Voices* was published in 1593; Dowland's *First Book of Songs* in 1597; Rosseter's *Book of Airs* in 1601, and Campion's *Two Books of Airs* in 1610. From his use of music (there are more than twenty songs in the plays, and dances are often an integral part of the action), and from the part it played in his imagery, it is clear that music meant as much to Shakespeare as books did.

But merely to talk about architecture, pictures and music is more useless than merely to talk about books. You can see some photographs of houses and works of art in Eric Mercer's *English Art 1553-1625* (*The Oxford History of English Art*); you can hear plenty of the music by listening to some of the following records (the numbers are for mono-versions):

Music of Shakespeare's Time, CLP 1633 and 1634.
Shakespeare Songs and Lute Solos, ALP 1265.
Music of Sixteenth Century England, TFL 6022.
Church Music of Tallis and Weelkes, RG 237.
Church Music of William Byrd, RG 226.
Church Music of Orlando Gibbons, RG 151.
English Music of the Early Seventeenth Century, AXA 4515.

ENGLISH RENAISSANCE DRAMA

Because any writer at the beginning of his career learns his job mainly by working within the tradition established by his predecessors in the same medium, we need to treat early Elizabethan drama, as a particular aspect of Renaissance culture, in more detail. We have said that Shakespeare on the whole wrote in the tradition of the popular, professional drama, and this is what we must illustrate most fully.

In Shakespeare's lifetime, the mediaeval plays on Biblical subjects—miracle plays—were still being performed; in fact he himself could have seen performances in Coventry before 1580. But neither these plays nor the village 'mumming' plays were as important in the development leading to Elizabethan drama as the professionally performed morality plays or 'interludes' (a term which seems to have been used in Tudor times to describe any sort of drama). These plays were didactic, at first dealing with personified abstractions, and nearly all concerned with the struggle between the forces of good and evil for the possession of a human soul (this struggle is known as the 'psychomachia'). In their popular form they were often deliberately constructed for small travelling troupes of five or six players; they contained many parts that could be doubled; they needed very little staging, and they tended to be episodic hotch-potches, with the abstract moral argument enlivened by song and dance, obscenity, and comic knockabout routines; in their performances the actors always showed themselves aware of the presence of an audience, sometimes addressing themselves directly to it.

By the 1560's and '70's the themes of these interludes had become secular rather than religious, material from historical chronicles and fabulous romances as well as from the Bible being used, while 'real characters' began to replace the abstractions. These later forms are sometimes known as hybrid-moralities, because allegory and realism ran side by side in parallel plots in the same play. Texts for about a dozen of these dramas are still extant; the most famous of them are Preston's *Cambises* (c. 1561) and Pickering's *Horestes* (1567). The first is particularly important because it gives a very good idea of the atmosphere of these early plays; also because Shakespeare may well have seen it performed in Stratford, and it is referred to by Falstaff in *1 Henry the Fourth*, as well as being the probable target of the satire in the play-production scenes in *A Midsummer Night's Dream*.

Recent scholarship has stressed the importance of these hybrid-moralities as the real link between mediaeval and renaissance drama, emphasising particularly Shakespeare's debt to their themes, structure and general approach. It certainly seems wiser to approach a Shakespearean play from something like *Cambises* than from modern realistic drama.

Not all moral interludes, however, were designed for the popular stage; more elaborate ones were written for special performance in more august surroundings, and by the time Shakespeare came to London there existed quite an extensive coterie, or élite theatre. There were court plays like *Damon and Pithias* (1571) or *Apius and Virginia* (1575), often needing large casts and elaborate staging, often performed by boy-actors. There were university plays like *Gammer Gurton's Needle* (1575). There were classical plays, usually performed at the Inns of Court. These last dramas were often modelled upon the Latin plays of Seneca, whose works had been published severally in the 1560's and all together in 1581. The most famous is the one now known as *Gorboduc* (1565), which will repay reading if only to illustrate the kind of play Shakespeare was *not* concerned to write (it is particularly useful to anyone studying *King Lear*).

These productions of a highbrow theatre cannot have meant very much to Shakespeare—although some court-plays were also given public performances, and plays like *Love's Labour's Lost*, *The Comedy of Errors* or even *A Midsummer Night's Dream* seem to have affinities with, for example, the work of Lyly (*Campaspe*, *Sappho and Phao*, *Gallathea*, *Endimion*) which was produced at court and in private theatres in the 1580's. We come nearer to Shakespeare's own work, both in spirit and in time, in the plays of Peele (*The Arraignment of Paris*, *The Battle of Alcazar*, *David and Bethsabe*, *The Old Wives' Tale*) and of Greene (*Orlando Furioso*, *Alphonsus*, *Friar Bacon and Friar Bungay*). These were performed, mainly by adult-companies in the public theatres, in the late eighties and early nineties. But the main achievement of the popular theatre, before Shakespeare, came about 1587 when Kyd's *The Spanish Tragedy* and Marlowe's two-part *Tamburlaine the Great* were first performed (*The Jew of Malta* and *Doctor Faustus* were also performed by 1590). If we add to all these three anonymous plays—*Arden of Feversham* (1592); *The Famous Victories of Henry the Fifth* (1598, but performed before 1588); and *George a Greene* (1599, but regarded as an old play in 1593)—you will have a fair selection of what had been created by the time Shakespeare started writing.

On the 19th of February, 1592, a company known as The Lord Strange's Men began a season at The Rose. They performed in their first fortnight, as well as six plays now lost, Greene's *Orlando* and *Friar Bacon*, Kyd's *Spanish Tragedy*, and Marlowe's *Jew of Malta*; on the 3rd of March they performed a play called *Henry the Sixth*—which may be one part of Shakespeare's trilogy. Within the next six years Kyd, Peele, Greene and Marlowe were all dead, leaving Shakespeare with no rivals, at least from the older generation of writers.

In 1590, when Shakespeare was twenty-six, of the dramatists we think of as Shakespeare's contemporaries, Chapman was just in his thirties; Dekker, Heywood, Jonson and perhaps Middleton were in their late teens; Marston, Tourneur and Webster were schoolboys; Beaumont, Fletcher, Ford and Massinger were children.

THE POLITICAL AND ECONOMIC BACKGROUND

On a large-scale view, Shakespeare may have been lucky in that his lifetime fell within the near-century of comparative calm between the last blood-letting of the Reformation (the Marian persecutions, in which some three hundred people were executed because of their religious beliefs, ended only six years before his birth) and the opening of the Civil War (twenty-six years after his death). Shakespeare lived in the interval between the disintegration of the mediaeval church and the disintegration of the renaissance court which had replaced it as a centre of power and culture. Yet the disruptive tendencies were there in a society building itself on Protestantism and Capitalism—a society in which there were no police, no standing army, and no civil service, and which had to cope with the strain of enclosures, evictions, vagrancy and pauperism caused by an accelerating change in the country's economy.

Throughout Shakespeare's life there was the constant insecurity of a challenge, both internal and external, to the nationally established order. Also there was in the background, as a never-to-be-forgotten warning, that thirty-year period of civil war which ended with the Tudor victory at Bosworth in 1485—and which was the subject of Shakespeare's first plays, written probably with the deliberate intention of showing to the present the horror of a past which could only too easily be repeated. (During the first twenty-five years of his life, there was the constant possibility of upheaval on the death of a queen who refused either to marry or to name her successor.)

Despite the compromise of the 1559 Settlement (an attempt to define the nature of the English church which was unacceptable to all but one of the bishops of the time) there was the doubtful loyalty of the English Roman Catholics or Recusants: the Northern Rising was in 1569; the Pope's Bull excommunicating and deposing Elizabeth, while absolving Catholics from their allegiance, was in 1570; the first Catholic missionaries (Englishmen trained on the Continent) were landed in 1574; Mary Stuart, after nineteen years in the country as a focal point of unrest, was executed in 1587.

There was the less serious, but still irritating, problem of English Puritanism—a word which seems to have been first used in 1564 to describe those who wished to drive the English reformation, on Presbyterian or Calvinist lines, considerably further from Papist ceremonial than the point established by the Settlement. This movement was responsible for the Vestments Controversy of the early 1560's, the denial of episcopacy in the 1570's, the Admonitions to Parliament in 1571 and 1572, the Martin Marprelate pamphlet-war of 1588 and 1589, and the running attack on everything in the world of professional entertainment (see Chapter 2).

There was a complementary challenge from outside the country—that 'English Enterprise' which seemed imminent in the late 1560's when Spanish forces were in the Netherlands.

This challenge continued through the years of commercial and religious hostility to Spain: Hawkins's defeat at San Juan de Ulua was in 1568; Drake's treasure raids at Nombre de Dios were in 1572, and his plundering in the Pacific in 1578; the declaration of war was in 1585, and the Armada in 1588.

There were, finally, the Guise-Huguenot religious wars in France. The Bartholomew massacres, which horrified Protestant Europe, were in 1572, and were a warning as potent as that of the Wars of the Roses of what could happen in England if dissident elements were allowed to flourish.

These tensions continued in the later years of the reign. There were further plots to kill the queen (the Lopez affair was in 1594); more harrying of Catholic recusants, and executions of their leaders; recurrent invasion threats (Penzance was burnt by a Spanish landing-party in 1595). There was plague, near-famine, the economic strain of a prolonged war, and that much-feared vagrancy which brought about the Poor Law Codification of 1597. Abroad, the war against Spain continued: English forces were fighting in Normandy and Brittany throughout the 1590's; there was the attempted naval blockade of Spain, and the loss of *The Revenge* in 1591; there were the deaths of Hawkins and Drake during their Caribbean raids of 1595 and 1596, the Cadiz Expedition of 1596, the Islands Voyage of 1597; there was the failure of peace negotiations in 1600. In addition, after 1595 a critical situation developed with Tyrone and O'Donnell's rebellion in Ireland—a situation aggravated when Spain tried to land troops there in 1601. Above all, there was throughout the late 1590's the danger of Essex's growing irresponsibility and political ambition which culminated in his attempted rising in London of 1601. This was the rising in which Shakespeare's colleagues became involved when, at the request of some of Essex's followers, they produced a special performance of *Richard the Second* with its deposition scene. Finally, the end of the reign saw signs of that conflict between ruler and parliament (here over the problem of monopolies) which was to become critical forty years later.

It seems unnecessary to pursue the story further. As it

happened, there was no civil war when the queen died, but even by the time he was established in London, about to embark on a writing career that was to last for more than twenty years, Shakespeare could have collected enough evidence to suggest that vision of a social and moral order descending into chaos, that brutish challenge to 'civility', which we shall suggest is one of the central points of his work (see Chapter 6).

READING LIST

G. E. Bentley: *Shakespeare, A Biographical Handbook* (Yale PB, 1961).
S. T. Bindoff: *Tudor England* (Pelican PB, 1952)
M. St. C. Byrne: *Elizabethan Life in Town and Country* (Methuen PB, 1961).
B. Ford (ed.): *The Age of Shakespeare* (Pelican PB, 1955)
F. E. Halliday: *The Life of Shakespeare* (Pelican PB, 1963).
G. B. Harrison: *Elizabethan Journals* (Doubleday Anchor PB).
K. Muir (ed.): *Elizabethan and Jacobean Prose* (Pelican PB, 1956).
J. D. Wilson: *Life in Shakespeare's England* (Pelican PB, 1944).
Shakespeare Survey (C.U.P.), Vols. 3, 14 and 17, cover the material dealt with in this chapter.
Two volumes in the *British Life Series* (ed. P. Quennell, Batsford), *Life in Tudor England* and *Life in Elizabethan England*, are particularly good for their illustrations.

Texts

J. Q. Adams: *The Chief Pre-Shakespearean Dramas* (Cambridge, Mass., 1924). (Includes many of the texts mentioned, but may now be difficult to obtain.)
World's Classics: *Five Pre-Shakespearean Comedies; Five Elizabethan Comedies; Five Elizabethan Tragedies* (Oxford).
Everyman Library: Marlowe's plays, Jonson's (2 vols.), and a selection of Beaumont and Fletcher's (Dent).
New Mermaid Series: Most Elizabethan dramatists represented (Benn).
Revels Plays Series: Individual plays are appearing currently in scholarly editions (Methuen).
Regents Renaissance Drama Series (Arnold PB).

2

Shakespeare's Theatre

The part of Shakespeare's world which, it is reasonable to suppose, affected him most materially was the one in which he earned his living—the London professional theatre. Many aspects are worth study: the relationship between the theatre and the authorities; the building of the playhouses; the conditions for which Shakespeare wrote; the effect of these conditions on his plays; and the implications of all this for a modern reader.

THEATRE AND AUTHORITY

Help from the court, and attempted repression from the Puritan-dominated Corporation—that is the background against which the London theatre developed between 1576 and 1642. The new entertainment industry became, in fact, a party to a much more extensive struggle between the ideals of a humanist renaissance and a Calvinist reformation, between the political aims of the aristocratic, centralising Privy Council (a group of the most important officers of the state) and those of middle-class local government.

Generally the court saw to it that the theatre continued to exist during these years. It did this partly because of the personal pleasure in play-watching taken by Tudor and Stuart rulers, partly because many leading courtiers were themselves patrons of acting-troupes, and partly because of jealousy of growing Puritan influence. But the court also saw that the theatre must be regulated. For example, as early as 1559 a Royal Proclamation gave local officials the task of licensing plays to be performed in their areas, and of forbidding any play 'wherein either matters of religion or of the governance of the state shall be handled or

25

treated'—these being concerns too serious for any men but those of 'authority, learning and wisdom'. In 1581 this duty was taken over by the Master of the Revels (an official responsible for providing court-entertainment); he was required to 'order and reform, authorise and put down, as shall be thought meet or unmeet', plays, players, play-makers and playing-places. In 1607 the same official took over from the ecclesiastical authorities the licensing of printed plays.

The Puritans wanted to stop rather than merely control plays. To them the theatre was a 'a consistory of Satan', and their arguments against it were expressed in many books. The general tone of the attack is well caught in a letter of 1597, from the Corporation to the Privy Council, asking for 'the present stay and final suppressing' of stage-plays in and about the City (you will find the whole document reprinted in *Life in Shakespeare's England*—see the reading list to Chapter 1):

> We have signified to your Honours many times heretofore the great inconvenience which we find to grow by the common exercise of stage-plays. We presumed to do so . . . being persuaded . . . that neither in polity nor in religion they are to be suffered in a Christian commonwealth, specially being of that frame and matter as usually they are, containing nothing but profane fables, lascivious matters, cozening devices, and scurrilous behaviours, which are so set forth as that they move wholly to imitation and not to the avoiding of those faults and vices which they represent.

In the end, of course, the 'final suppressing' came under the Roundheads in 1642.

For Shakespeare and his colleagues, this Puritanism probably represented little more than a nuisance—the kind of nuisance exemplified in the famous regulations of 1574 which applied to public playing-places within the City (no performance of improper or seditious plays, or of any play until licensed; similar licensing of playing-places and their controllers; no admittance to playing-places during divine service on Sundays or on holy-days). Even when regulations were enforced, ways round them could usually be found; in any case the theatres in which Shakespeare mainly worked, since they were built outside the City limits, were beyond the Corporation's jurisdiction.

But one aspect of play prohibition which was more serious was the closing of theatres in times of plague. Within the limits of Shakespeare's writing career, there was little playing in the winter of 1592, and virtually none from the end of January, 1593, to June, 1594—an eighteen-month closure which destroyed the organisation of many companies. Between 1603 and 1610 plague was endemic in London, usually lasting from July to November, at its height in the autumn. All the companies could do at such times was to travel in the provinces or even abroad.

Our own view of the Elizabethan theatre as a booming industry would at many times have appeared strange to those working in it.

THE THEATRES

When Shakespeare entered the senior part of Stratford Grammar School (somewhere about 1575, when Elizabeth had been queen for seventeen years) there were no specialised, public theatres in London. Plays were performed, as they had been for decades, by troupes of professional actors at court, in private houses or semi-public halls, and in the open air.

At court the festival season extended from November to the beginning of Lent, but plays were mainly performed during the twelve-day period of Christmas. Acting companies might be invited by the Revels Office to submit plays from their current repertoire and, if they were approved, to perform them (after special rehearsals) before the highly select audience in whatever royal palace the ruler happened to be. From 1558 to 1575 there were over seventy-five such performances, more by boy than by adult companies, and the fee for each performance was between £6 and £10. (There is a very vivid evocation of a court performance in Dr. Hotson's *The First Night of 'Twelfth Night'*.)

A company might be asked to perform in the hall of a great house, or of such an institution as the Inns of Court, to celebrate a special occasion like a wedding or a royal visit (*A Mid-*

summer Night's Dream and *The Comedy of Errors* may have been specially written for this type of performance).

Most important to the development of a public theatre were the open-air performances, given on a temporary trestle-stage, or on a waggon known as a 'pageant', wherever there was a convenient open space—the village-green, the market-place, the bull-baiting ring and, above all, the inns whose yards and galleries made a good auditorium. The first recorded performances in these inn-yards date from before Shakespeare's birth; they continued to be used in London, especially in winter because of their central position, well after the erection of proper theatres. In some cases the stage may have become a permanent feature of the yard, and the inn virtually a theatre, hired for a given period by an acting company.

Here already can be seen the basis of the two forms to be taken by the specialised theatre after 1576—the so-called 'public' (open-air, daylight) and 'private' (roofed, illuminated) playhouses. This distinction is more convenient than fundamental, for the same company could perform the same play, perhaps with slight alterations, at both types; and although the private theatre was more expensive, it was as 'public' as the other to those who could afford it.

In 1590 (to keep to the round figure for the beginning of Shakespeare's career suggested in Chapter 1) there were four public theatres in London, all deliberately built outside the City Limits, as the plan shows. The Theatre (1576) was used by several companies, but seems to have been a temporary home for Shakespeare's group between 1594 and 1596; The Curtain (1577) was probably used by Shakespeare between 1597 and 1599; Newington Butts (*c.* 1580), too far south of the river to be shown on our plan, was used by Shakespeare's group, in association with another, in July, 1594; The Rose (1587) was possibly the stage for which Shakespeare started to write, although it later became that of his chief rivals.

There had been a private theatre from 1576 to 1584 in the converted rooms of a disused Dominican monastery called Blackfriars, where public performances were given by a company

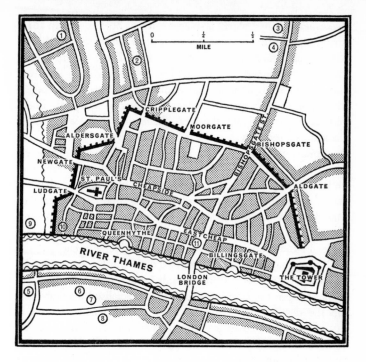

1. The Red Bull
2. The Fortune
3. The Theatre
4. The Curtain
5. The Swan
6. The Beargarden (later The Hope)
7. The Rose
8. The Globe
9. Whitefriars
10. Blackfriars
11. The Boar's Head

---

of boy-actors, as a preparation for court appearances. There was also a private theatre connected with St. Paul's, and used by the song-school from as early as the 1550's, but little is known about it.

In 1610 there were five or six public theatres. The Theatre and Newington Butts were out of action by 1598; The Rose was demolished *c.* 1606. The existing theatres were The Curtain; The Swan (1595) which may have been used by Shakespeare n the autumn of 1596; The Globe (1599) which was one of

Shakespeare's chief working-places—it was burnt down in 1613, during a performance of *Henry the Eighth*, and a second theatre of the same name was built on the site; The Fortune (1600) which was designed as a competitor to The Globe; The Red Bull (1604); The Boar's Head about which almost nothing is known, and which may have been a converted inn-yard. There were also two private theatres, Blackfriars and Whitefriars. Blackfriars (1600) was a second theatre in the rooms of the Dominican monastery, used at first by children's companies, but in 1609 occupied by Shakespeare's group as an alternative, winter, playing-place to The Globe (it is often argued that the use of this indoor theatre had its effect upon the nature of Shakespeare's last plays). Whitefriars was a theatre in the rooms of a disused Carmelite Priory; it was used by children's companies in 1608, but may have existed considerably earlier.

During Shakespeare's lifetime two more theatres were opened: The Hope (1613) and Porter's Hall (1615). Thus, in the forty years between the opening of the first specialised playing-place and the death of Shakespeare, there originated in London (a city of no more than 200,000 inhabitants) about a dozen theatres. To understand the way in which this theatre-building represented a booming entertainment-industry you might compare it with the growth of television companies in Great Britain during the last few years.

THE PERFORMERS

Acting troupes, apparently superseding the mediaeval minstrel-bands, existed long before there were any proper theatres ('interluders' appeared before Henry VI in 1427, and the Earl of Essex maintained a company in 1468). It was in fact only as a member of a troupe that an actor could operate. The free-lance performer of modern times was unknown, for to avoid charges of vagabondage an actor had to become legally a member of a nobleman's household. This he did by joining a company under the nobleman's patronage, wearing his badge and livery, looking to him not for wages but for protection. On the other hand, the patron was held responsible for the good conduct of his players, who performed of course wherever they could find an audience. Under these conditions the status of the adult-actor rose. Before 1590 he tended, at least in royal eyes, to be less popular than his boy-rival; by 1603, if a member of the leading companies, he could be a servant of the royal household, and even be given a place—as was Shakespeare himself—in the coronation procession.

From the beginning of Elizabeth's reign, acting-companies performed in London and the provinces, but their detailed history is confused. There may have been more than one group with the same name; a group sometimes changed its patron and therefore its title; companies amalgamated or exchanged personnel. The leading adult-companies (Leicester's Men until 1583; then The Queen's Men) were, however, already establishing the rhythm of theatrical existence: early spring to early summer in the London playing-places; late summer and autumn on provincial tours (inescapable at times of plague); early winter back in the capital to prepare for the climax of the year— the Christmas court-perfomances.

In 1590 the main adult companies were: The Queen's Men; The Admiral's Men, for whom Edward Alleyn created the leading roles in Marlowe's plays; and The Lord Strange's Men. It was apparently a nucleus from this last group that was reorganised, under the patronage of the Lord Chamberlain, after the 1593-4 plague epidemic. And it was this association (known as The Lord Chamberlain's Men until 1603, when it became The King's Men) that the thirty-year-old Shakespeare joined, remaining a member of it for the rest of his working life. How much The Chamberlain's and The Admiral's Men dominated the Elizabethan theatre can be seen from the records of court-performances: between 1594 and the Queen's death the former company appeared thirty-two, the latter twenty, and other adult-companies only five times. In the new reign The King's Men pulled far ahead of its rivals, and during the winter of 1604-5 no fewer than seven of Shakespeare's own plays were performed at court—as was the case again in the winter of 1612-13.

The Chamberlain's Men was organised as a joint-stock company: that is, the main actors (five of them at first, later increasing to twelve) bought a common stock of plays, properties and costumes, sharing part of the box-office income in proportion to their capital investment. Because they had bought such a share or part of a share, these men were known as 'actor-sharers'. There were two other kinds of actor in the company: perhaps about half a dozen 'hired men' who worked for a weekly wage, and the boy-actors apprenticed at the age of ten or so to the sharers. It was these boys, not to be confused with the members of the children's companies, who were responsible for the female roles, as no women (at least as far as English companies were concerned) appeared on the Elizabethan stage. One of the actor-sharers was appointed business-manager, and there would be some hired back-stage and front-of-house staff. There would be a book-keeper, responsible for the company's collection of plays, the prompt-book, the 'plot' and the individual 'parts'; the tire-man, responsible for the very expensive wardrobe; the 'gatherers' who, at various parts of the theatre, collected the admission-money in their boxes; the stage-keeper who kept the playing-area tidy; and the musicians (perhaps employed more in private than in public theatres). Presumably some of these men could be called upon as extras when needed, and the total man-power of a company would be about thirty. How closely Shakespeare's company was disciplined we do not know, but The Admiral's Men, under the close control of Henslowe—whose diary is the main source of our knowledge of Elizabethan theatrical affairs—had a system of fines for drunkenness, unpunctuality and so on. At first the group played in any available building, the owners of which received a percentage of the takings (usually half the gallery-receipts) as rent. In all this The Chamberlain's Men was similar to the other companies.

What distinguished the organisation after 1599 was that its new theatre, The Globe (and the same is true later of Blackfriars, when the company became the first adult one to perform regularly in a private theatre), was itself partly owned by some of the actor-sharers, who were then also known as 'housekeeper-sharers'. These men were thus responsible not only for the artistic policy of the group but also for such things as paying the ground-rent of the site, the licence-fee due to the Master of the Revels for the use of a theatre, local taxes, and the cost of maintaining the building. In return they took that part of the revenue which would otherwise have gone to an external landlord.

Shakespeare was an actor-sharer in the company by 1595, and for this share he would have to pay something like £30. In 1599 he bought, for anything between £80 and £100, one of the ten housekeeper-shares in The Globe. In 1608 he bought one of the seven shares in the Blackfriars theatre. Thus Shakespeare invested in the theatre for which he wrote, just as he invested in the property of his native town. He was a financially interested member of a compact and stable economic organisation.

All Elizabethan companies operated on a repertory basis, the long, continuous runs of our own system being unknown. Several plays (and the range in quality might be enormous) were given in any one week; a successful production would be given a second performance within a few days, and repeated at increasingly long intervals until the play faded from the repertoire; an unsuccessful one would simply be dropped, possibly after only one performance. Few plays appear to have remained in any company's repertoire for much more than a year; only two plays have more than thirty recorded performances, and it has been estimated that only ten per cent of all the plays achieved more than twenty. Twelve to fifteen performances could apparently be regarded as a fair success.

All this meant a tremendous consumption of material, as is the case with television drama today. Thus a group known as Sussex's Men, in the twenty-two days between January 16th and February 6th, 1594, gave twelve performances of nine plays, including the first performance of *The Jew of Malta* and of what seems to have been *Titus Andronicus*. Some scholars think that at the turn of the century there were about twenty full-time dramatists, each producing two or three plays a year; probably only a quarter of these plays were ever printed, and of the others

C

we know only their titles, if that. The companies were each introducing new plays into the system at the rate of about fifteen a year. The Admiral's Men, whose programme we know in detail, between 25th August, 1595 and 28th February, 1596 gave one hundred and fifty performances of thirty plays; only seven of these plays (given twelve performances) were more than a year old—and this seems to be a fair sample.

All this meant that in some cases mass-production methods had to be employed, with four or five dramatists working on one play, perhaps following a plot outline supplied by the company. As dramatists usually sold their work outright to a company for £6 or £7, there was considerable re-vamping of old stuff, over which the original author had relinquished control, by professional 'play-dressers'. It is from this incredible welter of material that there emerged the plays which we now study in such detail.

For the greater part of his career Shakespeare wrote for one group of actors (its members, of course, changed gradually over the years), and for it he created about thirty plays—half of them to be given in one theatre. He was in fact a kind of resident dramatist, able, as far as was possible within the system, to go at his own pace. Although his output seems large by modern standards, it was not particularly so by Elizabethan. Dekker claimed that between 1598 and 1600 he was entirely responsible for eight plays, and had contributed to twenty-four others—all for one company. Heywood in 1633 claimed 'either an entire hand or at least a main finger' in two hundred and twenty. Certainly Shakespeare had a more intimate, day-to-day concern with the profitable running of a playhouse than any other English dramatist at any time: he acted on its stage; he probably directed rehearsals, particularly of his own plays; he would have to attend business and administrative meetings with the other housekeepers. It is typical of the businesslike approach to playwriting shown by his company that when it moved into Blackfriars it brought in to write for it Jonson, Beaumont and Fletcher, who already had experience of indoor theatres.

What all this meant to Shakespeare as an artist, rather than merely as a dramatist concerned with making a living, is difficult to define. He worked for a known association of men, understanding their potentialities, preferences and mannerisms as actors; he knew the physical properties of the stage; he knew the number of men—and even perhaps the exact costumes and properties—that the company could call upon at any given time; he knew the theatre's audience, and its reactions. It is possible that future subjects for plays were discussed during the day's work; there is certainly evidence that competition with other groups often dictated the type of play a company was interested in. Shakespeare's plays, in fact, possibly from their conception were tailor-made for a particular cast—although we can now in most cases only guess at who played what. Some characters may well have been created because there was an actor who played that kind of part; obviously Shakespeare's fondness for the girl-disguised-as-boy situation is related to the fact that a boy was playing the girl's part in the first place.

Similarly, it is hard to define the reverse of this process: what alterations did the actors themselves suggest while rehearsing a play? This happens in any theatre putting on a new play, but it was presumably easier for the actors to worry out problems with the author when he was a financially interested member of their own group and rehearsing with them. Finally, we can only guess at the psychological effect on Shakespeare of his situation, but he must have been given confidence by the security and continuity of his working environment. It is useful to remember that Richard Burbage (son of the man who built The Theatre, and creator of many leading Shakespearean roles) joined The Lord Chamberlain's Men at the same time as the dramatist, and was remembered in his will twenty-two years later; that an original member of the group and its business manager, John Heminge, was a co-editor of the first collection of Shakespeare's plays nearly thirty years after his association with their writer had started.

THE STAGE

The interior details of Elizabethan public theatres are a matter of continuous scholarly controversy. At present the evidence (a copy of a drawing of The Swan, building specifications for The Fortune and The Hope, the chance comments of contemporary observers, and early stage directions) is not sufficient to provide clear answers. In any case it is unlikely that the arrangements were the same in different theatres; presumably later buildings incorporated improvements suggested by the deficiencies of earlier ones. Even less is known about the private theatres, which were smaller and more profitable. Some scholars think that the two kinds of theatre represent fundamentally different theatrical traditions, but their stage-structures were probably similar. Here we shall concentrate on the public stages —the places where most people saw most of Shakespeare's plays performed.

The non-acting areas can be quickly dealt with. There was an uncovered auditorium, in which for one penny the audience could stand on three sides of a projecting stage. This auditorium was small; anyone standing at the back was nearer to the actors than are the opponents to one another on the baselines of a modern tennis-court. There were also three galleries where, for additional charges, covered seating could be obtained—some of it in private 'rooms'. The capacity of such an arrangement has been estimated at between two and three thousand, an average audience possibly consisting of about a third of this. It seems likely that the interior of the theatre was quite elaborately decorated.

Most scholars think that the Elizabethan stage developed from the traditional, fairground 'booth-stage' which was basically like the illustration opposite.

When such a stage was erected as a permanent structure in a building modelled on the bull-baiting arena or the inn-yard, there was a basic pattern of three different playing-areas: open-, inner- and upper-stages (some writers suggest that in the early theatres there was a fourth area in a part of the auditorium itself). It may be suggested by the illustration on page 38.

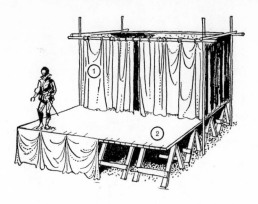

1. is the tiring-house, where properties were kept and actors prepared. From here entrances could be made either through the middle or at either end of the back curtain. By placing a ladder inside the tiring-house an actor could speak from above this curtain, thus making use of a kind of upper-level.
2. is the open stage, placed on temporary trestles, perhaps well above the heads of an audience which could stand on three sides.

It is the inner- and upper-stages that have caused most argument. Both seem to play an important part in Elizabethan staging: the one for such things as a tomb, a city-gate, a throne-room; the other for city-walls, balconies, upper rooms. But just how they looked and how they were used is not known. Some believe that both were recessed into the tiring house wall, and that considerable parts of the action might be performed there; some think that limitations on space and visibility precluded this. Some believe that scaffolding was brought on to the stage when an action 'above' was needed; some deny the existence of any inner-stage, arguing for a central entrance round which a tent or 'pavilion' could be placed. All may be right for different theatres, but the tendency of recent scholarship seems to be towards the opinion that as much of the action as possible was played on the open-stage.

One scholar (Dr. L. Hotson in *Shakespeare's Wooden O*) disagrees with the whole basis of this type of reconstruction,

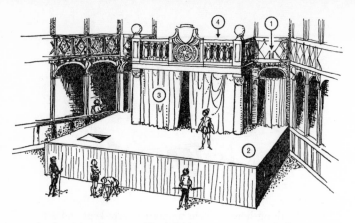

1. is the tiring-house wall, with three entrances as before.

2. is the open stage, rectangular or tapering slightly, projecting half-way out into the auditorium (The Globe's stage was probably just over forty feet wide and twenty-five feet deep), five or six feet high, boarded in or draped with curtains. There was usually at least one trap, giving an extra entrance from the under-stage 'Hell'. In some theatres the rear part of the stage was protected by a canopy (the 'Heavens'), highly decorated or hung with curtains to suggest the mood of the particular play being performed. Whether this canopy contained some sort of winch for spectacular descents and ascents is not known. When such a canopy was supported by two pillars, more variety was given to this main playing area, for these could serve as hiding places, or pivots round which action could move. On this open stage, tents (known as 'houses') may have been used to represent different localities (this technique—known as 'simultaneous setting'—was certainly used at court).

3. is the inner-stage ('study', 'discovery place' or 'enclosure') with curtains.

4. is the upper-stage ('chamber' 'the above').

---

because he does not believe in the presence of any tiring-house wall. He argues that the Elizabethan stage developed not from the booth-stage but from the wagon or 'pageant' stages on which the miracle plays were given, as he thinks, 'in the round'.

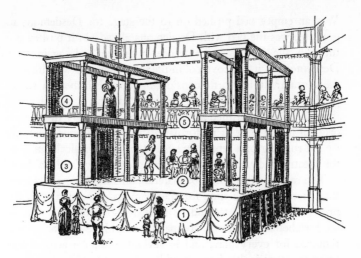

1. is the tiring-house, now in the under-stage, serving the platform by traps.
2. is the usual platform stage, now much less important.
3. is an inner-stage, opposed to another inner-stage, both having completely retractable curtains, manipulated in full view of the audience by stage-hands.
4. is the complementary upper-stage.
5. is where the best seats were to be found—in a gallery and on the stage itself.

Working on the assumption that two of these wagons were used together—as they were in contemporary Spain—he suggests a development leading to something like the illustration above.

Few scholars have been able to accept this pattern, but it certainly makes a stage as exciting in its variety and playing-possibilities as anything we have today.

THE STAGING

Those who make Elizabethan stage-conditions their special study are faced by such problems as the one presented in a Folio stage-direction: 'Enter Othello, and Desdemona in her bed'.

Was an empty bed pushed on to the stage for Desdemona to get into; was the bed with Desdemona already in it pushed out through the inner-stage entrance; was the bed, again with Desdemona in it, 'discovered' in the inner-stage by withdrawing the curtain? It is worth considering how Elizabethan stage-production (and behind that, perhaps, the plays as we know them, because the printed text may be a revision of the dramatist's original in the light of performance) was conditioned generally by the running of a repertory system, by the physical nature of the theatre, and by the styles of acting currently fashionable.

The rapid consumption of material, already discussed, meant that there was little time for the glamour associated with the present London theatre and its intensively prepared actors. In an Elizabethan repertory company probably every actor was required for every play, and in several roles. An actor might have to carry in his head anything between thirty and forty parts, which covered a very wide range. New productions—and we have seen that they were many—were prepared within a week or two of the company's receiving the script. A few rehearsals were presumably held in the mornings, with that minimum of fuss possible where there are no sets to get ready and mount, no lighting-plots demanding their own rehearsals, no intricate crowd-scenes, ensemble playing or elaborate business to plan. Perhaps there was very little 'production and direction' as we know it. The actor, once he got his individual part and cues, may have been left to work up his role by himself, with only one or two group-rehearsals. (It is interesting to notice that in Shakespeare's Globe plays most scenes involve fewer than five speaking-actors simultaneously.) Also the same effects, properties and costumes could be used in play after play, where in any case stock situations tended to recur—the siege-scene which played so well on the open- and upper-stages, or the overhearing-scene which used the pillars or an inner-stage. At least it was possible for The Lord Chamberlain's Men to perform at one day's notice (on Saturday, 7th February, 1601) Shakespeare's *Richard the Second*—a play not in their current programme.

The basic fact to grasp about this staging is that the Elizabethans never needed to pretend the theatre was not a theatre. Going to see a play was going to see just that: listening to words declaimed, watching actions performed by men moving about on a wooden platform which with its lack of scenic backcloth and its obvious, permanent structural features, must always remain a platform in a theatre.

Performances in public theatres took place for two or three hours during afternoon daylight, before an audience at least part of which would show the noisiness and restlessness of any standing group. There was no means of focusing attention from a darkened auditorium on to a sharply lighted stage. The audience was not isolated from the make-believe by distance or a front-curtain, or removed from the actor by footlights and orchestra pit. The repertory system made it difficult to forget that an actor was anyone but himself merely performing a role different from the one of yesterday and the day before. Perhaps what emphasised the theatricality of this theatre more than anything else was the way a play was introduced and concluded. Three trumpet-blasts announced a Prologue who gave out the title of the piece, and the entertainment (whether it was *Twelfth Night* or *King Lear*) was rounded off by a jig—not merely a dance, but a kind of short, usually obscene, comic opera. The effect seems similar to that produced by commercials in the intervals of television programmes.

Because this was a theatre to which 'realism' meant nothing, the dramatist could make great demands on his audience's credulity. The most obvious examples of this are what are known as 'localisation' and 'successive staging'—the way in which the stage was made to represent a particular series of places. The setting of a scene in an Elizabethan play was in any case often vague: it was enough if the audience knew it was in 'Rome' or 'The City of Troy' or 'The Forest of Arden' (compare this with the elaborate descriptions of a particular sitting-room in a particular house you will find in, say, the stage-directions of a play by Shaw). The lack of a painted backcloth meant that the platform physically represented nowhere—which meant in turn that it could be made to represent anywhere the writer mentioned. Perhaps one door was one town, a second door another; perhaps the inner-stage was one place, the upper-stage a second and the open-stage a third. Localities could be established simply by a character's saying where he was; they could be changed by a character's announcing he was going on a journey, walking a few yards, and declaring his arrival in a place which the stage now became. When in *King Lear* Edgar soliloquises while Kent sleeps in the stocks behind him (2, *3*), it does not mean that the two characters are in the same place; the audience either regarded the stage as two different places at once, or, more likely, pretended that Kent was not there. Some scenes take place nowhere at all, and this makes no difference to their impact. It has been well said that in an Elizabethan play a character enters primarily to another character, and not into any very particular place.

The stage's geographical flexibility, reinforced by the absence of a front-curtain, meant that the scene- and act-divisions which seem so definite in our printed texts were of little importance in performance. The action flowed quickly and continuously, as the stage was emptied of and filled again with actors (we do not know if there were intervals in the public theatres). Such speed and continuity meant that other liberties could be taken with an audience caught up in the impetus of the action. Time, for example, in Elizabethan plays is often as vague or as self-contradictory as the locale; the time-scheme of *Othello* does not make sense, but this would not be noticed in a performance.

Yet the platform so unconcerned with space and time, without lighting or extensive scenery, was not necessarily bleak and bare. The Elizabethans, as is obvious from their dress and their love of pageantry, enjoyed using their eyes, and they were encouraged to do this in the theatre.

There were the coloured curtains and hangings used about the stage; there were the notoriously splendid costumes, which had to stand up to daylight conditions, and which in some cases cost more than the play of which they were a part. The actual costuming of a play on the Elizabethan stage is another example of the audience's willingness to make concessions foreign to us. Certain main roles such as Greeks, Romans and Eastern characters seem to have had more or less accurate clothing, but the minor roles were given Elizabethan dress. We would accept either historical or contemporary dress, but not a mixture of both in the same play. There were also the properties which were a substitute for a painted backcloth. There is a famous list of those used at The Rose in 1598 which includes a rock, three tombs, a cage, a hell-mouth, the city of Rome, a bed and a bay tree. And this visual appeal was supported by plenty of noise when needed: trumpets, bells, thunder, explosions and music.

Despite this, the platform stage was one above all from which words were spoken; this was an aural rather than a visual theatre. One scholar, in fact, has estimated that, of the 345 scenes, in the fifteen plays Shakespeare wrote for The Globe, eighty per cent require nothing for their effects but a bare space, some actors and an audience.

How the all-important words were uttered, what the style of acting was like, again is a matter for scholars to argue about. It seems likely that the acting was ceremonial rather than realistic; the emphasis might have been on an individual reciting a part, playing much more directly to the audience than we would like. The delivery we may have found over-rhetorical; detailed acting and elaborate business might have been lost on a large stage, parts of which it was difficult to see from some places in the auditorium. This ceremonial acting, aided by the kind of conventional gestures and attitudes we associate with mime and ballet, would be consistent with the 'staginess' of the stage. Perhaps also it was only with some such style that a boy-actor could cope with the portrayal of Beatrice, Cleopatra or Miranda. It may be, of course, that acting-styles changed during Shakespeare's career, and that as his own blank verse moved away from the ceremonial set-speech to something much more conversational, so did the acting move away from the bombast which was so displeasing to Hamlet. It may also be that the style differed from theatre to theatre, possibly even from play to play. A louder, more emphatic style was needed at The Globe than at Blackfriars.

We have tried to stress two main points about how a play was staged at The Globe. This was a theatre of convention rather than of realism; situations were made as credible as possible, but credibility was never an end in itself, and the audience was prepared to play at make-believe far more than most modern audiences. This was a theatre of language rather than of spectacle; it was an actor's and writer's stage, not a producer's.

SHAKESPEARE'S PLAYS AND THEIR STAGE

It is possible to exaggerate the extent to which Shakespeare's work was controlled by the theatrical conditions for which it was written. The fundamental nature of a play—the conflict of characters and moral values expressed through dialogue—has not changed since The Theatre was erected. That Shakespeare's plays are not limited by their original environment is suggested by the fact that we still go to see them being performed in a very different kind of theatre, and by the fact that while the parts of Richard III, Hamlet, Lear and Othello were probably written with Burbage in mind, they show none of the similarities one would expect if they were all merely vehicles for one man.

Clearly Shakespeare enjoyed using the resources of his stage. This you can see in his use of the upper-stage (as the walls of Orleans in *1 Henry the Sixth* or of Harfleur in *Henry the Fifth*, or of Flint Castle in *Richard the Second*; as Silvia's window in *Two Gentlemen of Verona*, Juliet's balcony, Cleopatra's monument); in his use—more doubtful—of the inner-stage (Friar Lawrence's cell in *Romeo and Juliet*, Malvolio's prison, Edgar's hovel, Prospero's cave); in his use of the trapdoor (the graves in *Hamlet*, the descending apparitions in *Macbeth*). This you can also see in the exciting, spectacular events that he makes happen on the open-stage: the armed combat in *King Lear*, the duel in *Hamlet*, the wrestling-match in *As You Like It*, the funeral procession in *Titus Andronicus*, the dancing in *The Winter's Tale*, the bustling about in any of the battle-scenes.

Shakespeare also seized upon the freedom a conventionalised

44

theatre gave him. The soliloquy, the aside inaudible to another character, the slander instantaneously believed, the impenetrable disguise assumed merely by a change of costume or the putting on of a false beard—all these he knew the audience would accept, and all these he could use to keep the action moving or to give it a particular emphasis. He employed with tremendous effect the geographical flexibility of the stage, and the pace which resulted from the possibility of playing a series of short scenes uninterrupted by scene-changing; *Antony and Cleopatra*, for example, has fifteen scenes in Act 4, one of them only four lines long.

The ending of a Shakespearean play is one of the most obvious ways in which a drama was regulated by stage-conditions. The absence of a front-curtain made an ending at a climax (on what we would call a 'curtain-line') impossible. In the tragedies, for example, there had to be a certain relaxation at the end; over the dead bodies there had to be a pause, some speech-making—and then a funeral procession as in *Hamlet*. Apparently not even an Elizabethan audience was prepared to accept a convention by means of which a dead body could get up and walk off.

What is much more fundamental than any of the points we have so far made is that of the predominance of language in the Elizabethan theatre. The platform, we have said, was above all one from which words were spoken, and what this meant to the man who could do more with words than anybody·else in English literature before James Joyce needs no elaboration. Shakespeare's audience was prepared to listen, whereas we are prepared to watch. If its members were far less widely read than we are—even if they were illiterate—this probably meant that their ears were far more sensitive to spoken language than ours. This was the time when the sermon was still a major form of discourse, and when rhetoric, or learning how to make a speech, was an important part of grammar and university education. We hardly need to say that the language is important in a play by Shakespeare, but if you merely listen to, rather than watch, a play like *Much Ado About Nothing* what will strike you is the tremendous gusto in the manipulation of words: the obvious playing with language for comic effect, the variety of tone with which it is used, the variety of literary forms in which it is couched. Because Shakespeare's stage was what it was, the poet and the dramatist were able to come together in one work—and this leads us to a major problem with which to end this chapter and introduce the rest of the book.

THE TWO SHAKESPEARES

It is often said that Shakespeare never intended his plays to be read; he wrote them to be performed as stage-spectacles under certain conditions; if we take the plays out of this context we immediately falsify them. Yet reading him is what most of us students of Shakespeare do nearly all the time. We analyse him in the study more than we watch him in the theatre.

There are two Shakespeares. One Shakespeare is the man we have been discussing in this chapter. This is the dramatist whose work we speak of as 'coming alive' (with the implication that otherwise it is dead) in the theatre, when we go to watch the Royal Shakespeare Company or the local drama group—and by watching in this way we may have the experience of a lifetime. The second Shakespeare is the poet we encounter in what has been called the 'ideal theatre of the mind', and whom we analyse word by word.

We are not trying to answer the difficult question of what the relationship between these two Shakespeares should be, or to say that one is more interesting, or more valid, than the other. We are simply trying to make clear what we are going to talk about in the rest of this book.

The following chapters attempt to help you to read the second Shakespeare. This is largely the Shakespeare of examination syllabuses; it is certainly the Shakespeare discussed in most of the books in the reading lists. It is significant that some modern criticism refers to the plays as 'dramatic poems' which we must approach as we would any other printed poem. When you go to a theatre, or watch a play on television, you tend to sit back and watch a spectacle unfolding in front of you. You cannot hold up the action if anything catches your interest; you cannot really remember sufficient detail for any useful post-mortem. In any case what you have seen, particularly on television, is probably a version edited by a producer more interested in good theatre than in textual accuracy. Of course, the same thing happened in the Elizabethan theatre; many scholars think that *Macbeth* as we have it is an acting-version of a lost original. On the other hand, to *study* Shakespeare you must have a text, which you must get to know as well as you can; your tools are those of practical criticism and the exposition of ideas.

Polonius once asked Hamlet what he was reading. The reply was 'Words, words, words'. To these words—how they have been recorded, how Shakespeare manipulated them, what they seem to mean—we now turn.

READING LIST

B. Beckerman: *Shakespeare at the Globe* (Macmillan, New York PB, 1962).

M. C. Bradbrook: *Themes and Conventions of Elizabethan Tragedy* (Cambridge PB, 1960).

M. C. Bradbrook: *The Rise of the Common Player* (Chatto, 1962).

I. Brown: *How Shakespeare Spent the Day* (Bodley Head, 1963).

C. W. Hodges: *The Globe Restored* (Benn, 1953).

L. Hotson: *Shakespeare's Wooden O* (Hart-Davis, 1959).

A. M. Nagler: *Shakespeare's Stage* (Yale PB, 1964).

Shakespeare Survey, Vols. 1 and 12, deal with the theatre.

J. B. Styan: *Shakespeare's Stagecraft* (Cambridge UP, 1967).

G. Wickham: *Early English Stages*, Vol. 2 (Routledge and Kegan Paul, 1963).

3

Establishing the Text

Every student of Shakespeare is faced with a specific and, we believe, a very important question: can we be sure that the words we study are the words actually written by Shakespeare? This question cannot be answered satisfactorily without going into others: how plays were printed; what is the meaning of such terms as Quarto and Folio; how the early editors made guesses at Shakespeare's meaning; and how Shakespeare spelt and punctuated. Finally, there is the perennial question of the authenticity of the plays.

NECESSITY OF TEXTUAL CRITICISM

When, in the course of reading the second Shakespeare we mentioned at the end of the last chapter, you are looking up the meanings of obsolete words in a glossary, or consulting notes on obscure passages, you will often find such symbols as 'Q1' and 'F2'; or a reference to Rowe, Malone or Johnson. What do these mean, and are they important?

Everyone would agree that if the plays are worthy of study, it is essential to know what Shakespeare actually wrote. If the words printed in our *Henry the Fifth* are very different from his, how can we be said to be reading Shakespeare's *Henry the Fifth*? You will discover, as you read on, why this is a real possibility. To take an example, when Mistress Quickly describes the death of Falstaff, she says:

> ... for after I saw him fumble with the sheets, and play with flowers, and smile upon his fingers' end, I knew there was but one way; for his nose was as sharp as a pen, and a' babbl'd of green fields.
>
> 2, 3, 15-19

Our view of the dying reprobate is thus sentimentalised into the picture of a rustic knight remembering the green fields and rural innocence of his youth. Sir Edward Elgar, who wrote a symphonic poem about Falstaff in 1913, includes a charming pastoral idyll in the middle of the boisterous music to symbolise this 'babbling of green fields' that amounted almost to a death-bed repentance.

But the earliest authentic edition of the play, the First Folio (1623), says:

> . . . for his Nose was as sharpe as a Pen, and a Table of greene fields.

This does not make any kind of sense to us in the twentieth century, and even in the eighteenth it was obscure. That is why the editor Lewis Theobald made the brilliant guess that 'a Table of greene fields' was a misprint for 'a' babbl'd of green fields'; and this emendation has been universally accepted.

However, in 1962 a book appeared—*Explorations in Shakespeare's Language*—in which Mrs. Hilda Hulme, from her knowledge of Elizabethan English, proposes a plausible meaning for the words of the Folio. If Mrs. Hulme is right in her suggestions, the passage is a very bawdy one, and completely destroys the picture we all have (which is so poignantly portrayed in Elgar's music) of a peaceful, innocent fading away. So our view of Falstaff's character is affected by an editor's guess, or a printer's error.

Again, in the quotation from *Antony and Cleopatra* which we use to illustrate Shakespeare's mature imagery (Chapter 5), the word 'spaniel'd' occurs at a crucial point:

> The hearts
> That spaniel'd me at heels, to whom I gave
> Their wishes, do discandy, melt their sweets
> On blossoming Caesar. . . .

4, 12, 20-3

Dr. Caroline Spurgeon, the original researcher into Shakespeare's imagery, tells us that the image of a dog licking its master's hand

D

in flattery is often linked in the plays with the image of candy, sugar or sweets melting. She says (*Shakespeare's Imagery*, p. 196) that the word is printed 'pannelled' in the Folio, but the emendation of Hanmer (see p. 57) 'must be right'. Now Mrs. Hulme has found several reasons why 'pannelled' could also be right; Shakespeare might very well have written it, and Hanmer's correction, that seems so apt and on which so much critical theory is based, is only a guess that we have got used to and therefore accept.

Another emendation, this time by Nicholas Rowe, that we all accept as part of the great speech of King Henry before Harfleur:

Once more unto the breach, dear friends, once more

is equally startling. The Folio (1623) says:

But when the blast of Warre blowes in our eares,
Then imitate the action of the Tyger:
Stiffen the sinewes, commune up the blood,
Disguise faire Nature with hard-fauour'd Rage

3, 1, 5-8

We all say 'summon up the blood', ever since Rowe first made this guess. But if new research shows that 'communitions' were fortifications in 1656, and the Latin verb *communio* is shown in a school book of 1578 (that Shakespeare must have used) to mean 'To fortifie; to make strong; to fense on all partes', then it is more than likely that he wrote 'commune up the blood'. Yet another modern editor suggests that 'commune' is a misprint for 'coniure' or conjure—which also makes sense.

How, then, can anyone say that textual criticism, with its talk of Q, F and previous editors, is not important? So we must examine the authenticity of the texts. Can we, in fact, be certain that Shakespeare actually wrote what is printed today? The answer is, briefly, no. But there are so many qualifications to this 'no' that it is misleading to say it at all; so we will consider it unsaid until we have explained all the qualifications.

THE QUARTOS

The first question to consider is, what prevented Shakespeare from publishing his own plays in his lifetime and seeing them through the press, as a modern author does? This is not an easy question to answer.

Of Shakespeare's thirty-seven plays, only eighteen were published in Quarto form in his lifetime. (The word Quarto denotes the size of the page, a sheet being folded twice to give four leaves about the size of an exercise book. Similarly, Folio means a book of a much larger page, a sheet being folded only once to give two leaves the size of a sheet of foolscap.) Six of these Quartos were not, in fact, genuine—in the sense that Shakespeare had any hand in their publication. They had probably been printed without Shakespeare's permission or even approval and are consequently very unreliable. Today we call them 'bad Quartos'.

It was not customary for plays to appear in print. It is thought that at least sixty plays were newly produced in the theatres of London each year; yet on the average only nine were published. The reason for this is clear enough: the plays were the absolute property of the company of actors who performed them. A playwright was paid less than £10 outright for the MS; and as the company would wish to keep exclusive rights in their property, they took great care not to let other companies get copies.

If a company broke up or went bankrupt, it might well save a little out of the wreck by selling its stocks of plays to other companies, or to a printer, who might give £2 for a play. After the disastrous plague years, 1593-4, several plays were sold by penniless actors; in 1594 eighteen Quartos of various authors were published, including two by Shakespeare. One of these, *2 Henry the Sixth*, was a pirated version.

Although it was not the custom to publish plays as a rule, Shakespeare's own company printed, as good Quartos of course, fourteen of his plays before 1610, while he was still probably in London and certainly closely associated with them. Two of these genuine versions were put out shortly after pirated editions had appeared—*Romeo and Juliet* and *Hamlet*. Four other Quartos were published, and for a long time scholars thought that the bad Quartos of *2* and *3 Henry the Sixth* were old plays which Shakespeare had to work on in writing his own plays.

How did these bad Quartos get into print? It used to be thought that they had been taken down in shorthand during performances; there were systems of shorthand invented at the time, so this is quite possible. One modern view is that they were worked up from discharged actors' memories of their parts —usually minor ones. A new theory is that the bad Quartos represent 'degenerate' versions of the plays, that had been performed so often on the stage (perhaps by second-rate touring companies) that many alterations had been made. Often the version produced is ludicrous (see the First Quarto facsimile between pp. 72–3). But it must have been a source of money to somebody. Discharged actors would join some of the many touring companies that made a precarious living in the provinces; and a play that they could pass off as Shakespeare's would draw the innocent rustics as the down-at-heel actor in *Huckleberry Finn* did, with his mangled *Hamlet:*

> Soft you now, the fair Ophelia!
> Ope not thy ponderous and marble jaws,
> But get thee to a nunnery, go!

The good Quartos were probably published in answer to the demand of educated persons; they were printed from playhouse copies with the approval of The King's Men, which was a powerful and protected organisation, and would not let its rights go by default. How far Shakespeare himself saw them through the press we cannot tell. He was kept far too busy in the theatre to have had much time for proof reading. He was writing more than one play a year, and it is the nature of all of us, particularly of creative minds, to be more interested in the new work than in tinkering with the old, or doing the boring chore of proof-reading.

There were, then, in Shakespeare's lifetime, twenty Quartos for eighteen different plays—fourteen good and six bad, two of which overlapped. The bad ones are pretty worthless, but the good ones pretty good. Several of them saw more than one edition, some of them as many as six, before 1623, when the First Folio was published. In each case, some previous printer's errors were corrected, but new ones crept in; hence no good Quarto, whether called Q1 or Q6, can be considered much superior to any other.

After 1623 further Quartos appeared, but they were merely copies of copies, with multiplying errors.

Shakespeare retired to Stratford about 1610 to live the life of a country gentleman. Why did he then not prepare for the press a definitive edition?

The short answer is that he died in 1616, not very long after he retired. In this very year his friend Ben Jonson published a complete edition of his own works, and it is interesting that he made extensive alterations in the text as previously published. Perhaps Shakespeare was intending to do the same, for he can hardly have valued his work as less worthy of posterity's interest than Jonson's. Indeed, in the introduction to the First Folio, in which Jonson is thought to have had a hand, the editors say:

> It had been a thing, we confess, worthy to have been wished, that the author himself had lived to have set forth, and overseen his own writings; but . . . he by death [is] departed from that right.

This probably means that he had the project in mind.

As it was, the first collected edition of the plays is the First Folio (1623), edited by two of the old sharers of the company in which Shakespeare had spent nearly all his theatrical life. They were John Heminge and Henry Condell; to them we owe a tremendous debt of gratitude, for they provided the more or less complete and authentic text of no fewer than thirty-six plays. Their edition has been much reviled by past editors. There are many obvious misprints, wrong numbering of pages (there are over 900 pages of double columns) and other faults incidental to publishing. Hence the two editors have been called ignorant actors who were cashing in on the reputation of the great

Shakespeare when he himself could not prevent them from putting out garbled versions. This view is reinforced by the remarks of Dr. Johnson (in his *Proposals for an Edition of Shakespeare*, 1756):

> He sold them, not to be printed, but to be played. They were immediately copied for the actors, and multiplied by transcript after transcript, vitiated by the blunders of the penman, or changed by the affectation of the player ... and printed ... from compilations made by chance or by stealth out of the separate parts written for the theatre ...

Naturally, if this view of the First Folio prevails, any editor will feel at liberty to alter and 'improve' in whatever way takes his fancy, and this is exactly what all editors up to recent times did.

But Heminge and Condell were far from being ignorant or dishonest. They were both churchwardens in London, men of high reputation among their fellow-citizens as well as in the acting profession, which was itself becoming eminently respectable—witness Alleyn's rise to the status of gentleman, his buying of the manor of Dulwich, his founding of Dulwich College, and his second marriage to the daughter of John Donne, Dean of St. Paul's. He and his fellows were obviously as 'respectable' as are today's theatrical Knights and Dames.

As for their being ignorant of literary merit, it is impossible to imagine that men with such experience in the theatre (for they had spent nearly thirty years, a period longer than Shakespeare's, in the same company) could be incapable of preparing an authentic edition of the plays of their greatest writer and intimate friend.

We now believe the First Folio to be a very creditable attempt to give Shakespeare to the world. So much is this so, that the presence of a play in the First Folio is now considered reasonable evidence that it is by Shakespeare, and much barren controversy is virtually at an end.

'FOUL PAPERS' AND 'PROMPT BOOK'

If, then, the First Folio is authentic Shakespeare, and the

fourteen good Quartos are also authentic, how does it come about that the two often differ quite considerably? To answer this it is necessary to go a little deeper into the ways of authors and actors, in order to determine what the actors actually had in their hands while they were learning their parts and rehearsing on the stage.

The author would write on large sheets of paper, with many corrections and crossings-out. These were called 'foul papers', because they were apparently handed in to the theatre in an incomplete and muddled state. Sometimes the MSS would be quite neatly copied by the author, but more usually they would be interlined and hard to read. Several such MSS survive; one in particular is of immense interest, for part of it is now thought to be an actual example of Shakespeare's handwriting. This consists of three pages containing 147 lines of a revised version of *Sir Thomas More*, a play by various unidentified authors; these pages read like Shakespeare's work, and are in a handwriting which agrees with his known signature (see the facsimile facing p. 72).

'Foul papers' such as these were sorted out and put to rights by the 'book-keeper', who may have been the producer of the stage performance. It is obvious that if Shakespeare was acting in his own plays, as a senior member of the company, he would not allow the cutting up of his work such as we read goes on in Hollywood. A clearly written acting version was produced, usually by an experienced theatrical scribe; this was called the 'prompt book', and was made up of separate sheets of folio size, sewn together. This was the copy which was sent to the Master of the Revels, whose 'allowance' was an essential condition of performance. This official could demand cuts and alterations, on political or religious grounds; hence the final version was often different from the author's first intentions—for this reason as well as for other obvious reasons such as changes of mind by the author, objections from the company, incapability of the performers, and box-office considerations.

Two equally authentic sources of Folio and Quarto are therefore possible: one, the author's 'foul papers', or first draft;

two, the 'allowed' prompt book. It is possible that the 'foul papers', preserved by the company, were used for the Quartos, while the prompt books were the basis, in the First Folio, of those plays which had not been previously published as Quartos. In any case, Heminge and Condell are thought to have used manuscript versions, preserved in the archives, to correct those Quartos—the good ones—on which they based their Folio. Some plays, for example *Antony and Cleopatra*, are printed direct from a MS possibly by Shakespeare himself.

All this is largely conjecture, though it is based on meticulous examination of the many texts, dozens of Elizabethan manuscripts, and a vast amount of bibliographical knowledge. The present state of opinion is: where there is a good Quarto, it is printed from the authentic sources; where there is no good Quarto (over half of the thirty-seven plays) the First Folio is authentic.

LATER FOLIOS

Just as the later Quartos added mistakes while correcting others, so the later Folios are badly emended copies of the First, and have no authority. The only point of interest is that the Third Folio (1663) added seven plays, only one of which is accepted as substantially by Shakespeare. This is *Pericles, Prince of Tyre*. Of the other six, *A Yorkshire Tragedy* is the most interesting but is not by Shakespeare. This Folio, and the Second and Fourth, had no connection with The King's Men.

EARLY EDITORS

It was not until the eighteenth century that any attempt was made to establish a clear text, and to do away with the many obvious muddles that Shakespeare himself cannot have been responsible for. In 1709 Nicholas Rowe produced the first complete edition, setting himself to emend the text of F4, which was sprinkled with the accumulated mistakes of several printers. Rowe claimed to have consulted earlier editions; he completed lists of characters, assigned speeches to the right speakers, and tidied up stage directions, many of which were at variance with the text. He made Shakespeare more intelligible, even if he made many guesses which have since been proved wrong.

Succeeding editors all added their own emendations in the same way, yet were in the habit of maligning each other's work while drawing heavily on it. The first scholarly edition was Lewis Theobald's (1733) which earned the abuse of Pope, who had brought out his in 1725. Theobald is the target of much scurrilous invective in Pope's *Dunciad*; it was quite unmerited, for Theobald's edition, unlike Pope's, drew systematically on the Quartos, contained references to Shakespeare's sources, and discussed the order in which the plays were written.

Based on Theobald's text were the editions of Hanmer (1744), Warburton (1747) and Johnson (1765). Dr. Johnson was, according to Boswell, too lazy to do the necessary collation of earlier texts; but his Preface is still well worth reading for its insight into the plays as literature.

By this time the works of Shakespeare were arousing scholarly interest; the sophisticated London and University reader wanted to know more about the great dramatist whose works were coming to be regarded not merely as barbarous effusions of a primitive age, but as the glory of our literature. Consequently the next editor, Capell (1768), explored Elizabethan and Jacobean literature as a whole, and made the first studies of original documents like the Elizabethan Stationers' Register of publications. This work goes on still; it seems that the more that is learnt about Shakespeare and his times, the more there is to comment on. We can thus sympathise with the next two editors, Steevens (1773) and Malone (1790), who read widely in Elizabethan literature yet were mocked for their scholarship. It was Steevens who said:

> If Shakespeare is worth reading, he is worth explaining; and the researches used for so valuable and elegant a purpose, merit the thanks of genius and candour, not the satire of prejudice and ignorance.

Malone claimed to have 'carefully examined the meanest of books' in order to find clues 'to explain his fugitive allusions to customs long since disused and forgotten'.

These praiseworthy labours had, unfortunately, the result that they were often directed towards justifying ingenious emendations, many of which—like 'a' babbl'd of green fields'—are now accepted. But modern editors, who see the good Quartos and the First Folio as nearer to Shakespeare's intention than anything since published, are discarding as many of these eighteenth-century emendations as they can. This process is aided by study of Elizabethan dialects and spoken English; and we now realise that if we do not understand Shakespeare it is because we are removed from him by nearly four centuries of time and a whole series of revolutions, scientific, industrial, political and social.

MODERNISATION OF THE TEXT

So far we have not touched on a most obvious difference between the Folio and our modern texts: that is, the spelling, punctuation and other conventions of the printing of plays.

Some people would prefer to read Shakespeare—as we do Chaucer—in the original spelling. The snag here is that we do not know how Shakespeare himself spelt. If the three pages of *Sir Thomas More* are truly written by him, he must have been a very odd speller indeed, and an even odder punctuater (see the facsimile and transcription facing p. 72).

It is said that Shakespeare was an 'old-fashioned' speller, and the Quartos and Folios are more likely to be in compositors' spelling, even if they were set up from original MSS; and it is certain that the same compositor would vary his spelling in order to 'justify' (fit into the given space) the lines. A constant modernisation of spelling has been proceeding ever since F2. How would you react to:

Full faddom five thy father lies

or

Macbeth does murther sleep

which is what the first editions printed, and what Shakespeare probably wrote?

58

The same process has gone on in the punctuation. Our modern methods are logical; that is, we split our sentences up into meaningful pieces—clauses or phrases—with commas to separate them. The punctuation in the early texts was more rhetorical; that is, it goes according to the voice. This can be illustrated by the difference between the way we say and the way we punctuate expressions like 'Please, sir!' The first lines of the F1 text of *Othello* are printed thus:

> Neuer tell me, I take it much unkindly
> That thou (*Iago*) who hast had my purse,
> As if ye strings were thine, should'st know of this.

However we might punctuate this today, it would not be in this way; but again, we cannot say this is the punctuation Shakespeare used. On the evidence of the *More* MS, he used hardly any stops.

Another interesting feature of the early texts is the haphazard way in which some words have capital letters, and some not. It has been suggested that the words so capitalised are the ones to be emphasised by the actor; but this is not at all systematic, as is clear from these lines of *King Lear*:

> Blow windes, & crack your cheeks; Rage, blow
> You Cataracts, and Hyrricano's spout,
> Till you have drench'd our Steeples, drown the Cockes.
> You Sulph'rous and Thought-executing Fires,
> Vaunt-curriors of Oake-cleauing Thunder-bolts,
> Sindge my white head.

3, 2, 1-6

ACT, SCENE AND LINE DIVISIONS, AND STAGE DIRECTIONS

It seems that Shakespeare's MSS did not clearly indicate the ends of Acts. The early Quartos had no divisions at all, and we do not know when the intervals were taken in the theatre of the time. Since there was no scenery to change, and little removing of properties to be done, there was no mechanical need for an interval as there is in most modern plays; neither could the audience troop into the bar, as there was no bar to go to. Probably drinks were sold during the actual playing, as they still are at the opera performances in, for instance, the Baths of Caracalla in Rome. In the Folio, however, most of the plays are divided into Acts and some into Scenes; it is thought that Ben Jonson set the fashion for this copying of the Senecan conventional divisions by his 1616 definitive edition of his works, and that in 1623 Heminge and Condell felt obliged to follow suit.

Various editors since then have tidied up the imperfect divisions of the Folio. The result is our logical modern system; but this is not the work of Shakespeare, as far as we know. There are still places, indeed, where the Act and Scene divisions break up the flow of a play or spoil a contrast.

Line divisions, too, are often different from what was printed in the Quartos and Folio; many prose passages, for example, turn out to be verse, and are now so printed.

Finally, the Stage Directions are rarely those of Shakespeare himself. Some are obviously the additions of the 'book-keeper' or prompter, inserted to help him to keep the performance running smoothly. When a company is used to acting together, and the author is present at rehearsal and in performance, there is little need for stage directions to be written down. So in the plays he wrote after joining The Chamberlain's Men, they are as short and functional as possible—so much so that we may well wish they had been fuller. For instance, in the 'nunnery' scene of *Hamlet* (3, 1) where Ophelia is 'planted' by the King and Polonius, who are hiding behind the arras, Hamlet asks, 'Where's your father?' Ophelia replies, 'At home, my lord.' At this point, or just before it, it is customary in stage presentations for Polonius to stir the arras or to reveal his presence in some other way to Hamlet, thus prompting the question. Ophelia's faltering reply shows her a liar. Hamlet's speech becomes more violent; from self-searching ('What should such fellows as I do crawling between earth and heaven?') he turns to abuse. What causes this sudden change but the realisation that he is being spied on, and that Ophelia is a decoy? Yet there is no stage direction here, only a long theatrical tradition.

Macbeth provides an interesting example of the difference

between stage directions and text. Everybody knows that the play tells of the prophecies of three witches, who appear from time to time throughout the story. Yet the word 'witch' never appears in the authentic text; it is not spoken, but appears only in the stage directions. There is a subtle difference between the idea of witches (black magic, cats and broomsticks) and the words Shakespeare wrote in the text—'weird Sisters'—instruments of Fate, a far more powerful conception.

In the last plays, when Shakespeare's connection with The King's Men was probably less immediate, the stage directions are fuller. We would expect this if he were living in Stratford and sending the plays up to London to be put on without his help.

Thus it is clear that we cannot be sure who wrote the stage directions, especially in the plays of the middle period, where they are sketchy in the extreme. As Dr. Johnson said, he wrote the plays to be acted, not read. A modern playwright hopes to have his plays read by thousands, and to this end he will include elaborate descriptions of the scene, and even details of the appearance of the characters. Long stage directions are probably a hindrance to the actors, but a great help to readers. Succeeding editors, from Rowe onwards, have inserted them, from bare scene localities to quite detailed actions.

OUR DEBT TO EDITORS

The attempt to give the world exactly what Shakespeare wrote still goes on. American editors are hard at work on a new line of approach: conditions in Elizabethan printing houses and the habits of the several compositors—whose work can be positively identified—who set up F1. Collating machines compare different printings of the same page, and fantastically detailed examinations of every available copy of the plays are meticulously carried out. It is rather amusing to read, in an early nineteenth century edition, that 'the text may now be thought to be fixed beyond the hope, or at least the probability, that any future discoveries will be able to add much to its purity'; for American editors now consider that even the best English editions, the result of devoted lifetimes of labour by our scholars, are little better than school texts.

The object of the modern editor is primarily to give us an intelligible Shakespeare, and our debt to all those who have contributed to this end can be easily assessed when we look at facsimiles of the Quartos and Folios. Consider this short extract from *King Lear*:

> Thou think'st 'tis much that this contentious storme
> Inuades vs to the skinso: 'tis to thee,
> But where the greater malady is fixt,
> The lesser is scarce felt. Thou'dst shun a Beare,
> But if they flight lay toward the roaring Sea,
> Thou'dst meete the Beare i' th' mouth, when the mind's free,
> The bodies delicate:

First Folio, 3, 4, 9-15

This does not make very good sense. Apart from misleading punctuation, there are two bad printer's errors. A good deal of the pleasure of reading Shakespeare would be lost if modern texts were as bad as this. So we should be thankful for three hundred and fifty years of Shakespeare scholarship.

AUTHENTICITY

Does it matter, in the last resort, who wrote 'Shakespeare's' plays? Whether the plays are his or not, they are still there for you to read, and they are the same plays, whoever wrote them (the best exposition of the problem is H. N. Gibson's *The Shakespeare Claimants*—see Reading List).

There is, however, another aspect of the problem. We know that *Henry the Eighth* was only partly Shakespeare's, and that he probably wrote only the last three acts of *Pericles*. We also know that when plays were revived in the theatre, and when they went on tour, they were subjected to revision; it is reasonable to suppose that the author was not always able to supervise, and that others contributed new scenes or speeches. Indeed the case for accepting as Shakespeare's handwriting the *Sir Thomas More* addition rests on such a supposition. We also know that Shakespeare based some of his own plays—*King John, Hamlet,*

Henry the Fifth, for example—on older plays which he used as sources, perhaps even incorporating passages from them into his own.

If all this is granted, some parts of what we accept as his may well not be so at all. During the last century several attempts were made to specify such passages. This process of 'disintegration' was carried to absurd lengths, but we can be sure that there are some few spurious portions. *Macbeth*, in particular, has suffered much revision, and a good case can be made out for rejecting all the speeches (with song and dance) of Hecate, some of the Witches' speeches, and even the whole of Act 1 Scene 2, where the bombastic style of the bleeding Sergeant and of Ross does not ring true to some ears—and doubt is reinforced by the difficulty of reconciling the statement about Macbeth fighting the Thane of Cawdor, 'that most disloyal traitor', with Macbeth's own remark, a few minutes later, 'The Thane of Cawdor lives, a prosperous gentleman'.

This line of study may be interesting, but it is profitless, since the texts we now have are generally accepted.

READING LIST

H. N. Gibson: *The Shakespeare Claimants* (Methuen, 1962).
W. W. Greg: *The Editorial Problem in Shakespeare* (Oxford, 1962).
Shakespeare Survey, Vol. 5, is concerned with textual criticism.
Facsimiles of the Folio, edited by J. D. Wilson (Faber).
Facsimiles of the Quartos, London Shakespeare Association (Sidgwick & Jackson).
Othello, New Variorum Edition (Dover PB, Constable, 1963), is a reproduction of F1.

4

Shakespeare's Language

Having shown how the plays came to be printed, and how much
we owe to scholarly researches into the text, we now turn to
Shakespeare's use of words, by which he will live on whether
his plays are performed well or badly, or not at all. First we look
at his command of the language of his time; and then examine
the development of his verse and his varied use of prose and
verse. The most fascinating aspect of all, his imagery, is dealt
with in Chapter 5.

SHAKESPEARE'S LANGUAGE

During the sixteenth century our language was undergoing a
tremendous upheaval. The impact of the 'new learning' was
being fully felt; hundreds of new words came into the language,
most of them taken direct from Latin. English was not yet quite
respectable as the language of scholars, who usually wrote in
Latin and could use that language as fluently as they spoke their
mother tongue. Latin, not English, was taught in schools. The
declared object of the pedagogues of such schools as Stratford
Grammar School was to make their pupils write, talk and even
think in Latin, for much the same reasons as the Classics are
studied today: not only was Latin considered an elegant and
learned language, but the works of the Latin authors were held
to embody a complete code of conduct which the young would
do well to adopt. Much of this literature was committed to
memory; hence at the foundations of Shakespeare's vocabulary
was a solid substratum of Latin prose, poetry and proverbial
sayings, all of which he shared with those of his audience who
had been to school.

He gives us an amusing picture in *Love's Labour's Lost* of a schoolmaster, Holofernes, who is made to say:

> Mehercle, if their sons be ingenious, they shall want no instruction; if their daughters be capable, I will put it to them; but, vir sapit qui pauca loquitur. [As he sees Jaquenetta approaching] A soul feminine saluteth us.

4, 2, 74-77

If schoolmasters spoke this mongrel language and expected to be understood, it is no wonder that educated men, such as the University Wits who wrote plays for a living, should also draw their vocabulary from Latin as they thought fit. For the language was not, in any sense of the word, fixed; apart from Anglo-French or Anglo-Italian vocabularies, there was no really good English dictionary until 1755, when Dr. Samuel Johnson produced his famous volumes. A single page of this momentous work has: *officinal, offuscate, oleose, olidous, olitory,* all of which have since died, and all of which are Latin in origin.

No language which is spoken by living people ever is, or can be, fixed. This we now recognise again after a period of 200 years, during which grammarians have vainly striven to resist all change. But in Shakespeare's time English was even more hospitable to new words than it is now. What an outcry there has been over words like *hospitalize* and *finalise,* though both these are now fully current in circles where they are needed every day. If speakers and writers, that is, you and I and the man next door, heeded what the resisters to new usages tell us, we should be condemned to a very limited vocabulary. Such resisters (among them Ben Jonson and Thomas Nashe) tried in Shakespeare's own time to kill such new words as: *conscious, jovial, notoriety, negotiation, reciprocal, spurious, clumsy, strenuous, conduce, method.*

Shakespeare, in spite of his mockery of Holofernes, was himself one of the greatest innovators. That is, many words appear in print for the first time in his plays; but we must always remember that these words may have been spoken before Shakespeare wrote them down; also that there must be many

E

printed and manuscript pages, now lost to us, which may have contained Shakespeare's 'new' words. Here are, however, some of those credited to Shakespeare: *aerial, auspicious, assassination, bump, countless, denote, disgraceful, eventful, exposure, fitful, gnarled, hurry, impartial, pedant, perusal, predecease, savagery, sportive.*

There are hundreds of other words, too; many of them have not lived. Shakespeare would invent one on the spur of the moment to express his meaning in the heat of composition. For instance, *fluxive* for 'flowing' and *deceptious* for 'false' are two which might very well have caught on, but for some mysterious reason were hardly ever used again, and have certainly not survived into our times.

The list above is made up mostly of Latinate words, but you will have noticed *bump* and *gnarled, fitful* and *hurry*. These words remind us that one source of Shakespeare's vocabulary was the language of the ordinary people, which he naturally used and extended, just as he used and extended the meaning of the learned vocabulary of the educated. As he was the first to call a happening an *event*, so he is responsible for our calling a road a *road*. Before and during his life, the usual meaning is 'raid', what we would call an 'inroad'. It was he who used it as the name for a street or paved surface leading from one place to another, as in *1 Henry the Fourth* where a tavern is described as: 'the most villainous house in all London road for fleas' (2, 1, 12). This must have been becoming current usage when Shakespeare wrote it; nevertheless, from it we may deduce that while he was in full command of scholarly, Latinised speech, he also had a keen ear for the racy, everyday English of the man in the street.

Dialect Words
Indeed, many dialect words from his native Warwickshire appear in his plays, often with immense effect. When Banquo's ghost appears, Macbeth says:

For the blood-bolter'd Banquo smiles upon me.

4, 1, 123

66

'Boltered' is a West Midlands word meaning 'clotted', and Shakespeare must have heard it in Stratford. The mad Lear says to the eyeless Gloucester: 'Dost thou squiny at me?' (4, 6, 137); and the gods in the same play keep a 'pudder o'er our heads' (3, 2, 50). Such dialect words tell us that even when he was the favourite poet of courtiers and scholars he was still at heart a country lad; also that in his day the metropolis had not grown so self-important that men from the provinces had to ape the South-Eastern speech of the Londoner, as they do today. There was none of this U and non-U business, and the range of permissible accents was far larger than it is today. We are told that Sir Walter Raleigh spoke broad Devonshire all his life. Since Shakespeare never severed his own connection with Stratford, we may be sure that he, too, spoke with a Warwickshire burr in his voice and used the expressive words of his own folk, in the unpretentious manner that, on the evidence of his friends, we associate with him.

It is inevitable, indeed, that a dramatic language such as Shakespeare's, which has its roots in the life of the community, should include words from dialectal and vulgar sources. It is part of Shakespeare's universal appeal. 'The limits of my language,' said the philosopher Wittgenstein, 'are the limits of my world.'

Not only single words are attributable to Shakespeare, but also many expressions which may well have been proverbial in his day, and common in the spoken language. Many people were then illiterate; they were not hide-bound by the printed word, as we are today. This made for an increased vividness of language, and a greater relish of the spoken word (see p. 45). The Elizabethans were willing to accept and tolerate more than we can, with our artificial and often ridiculous conventions (such as printing 'don't' as 'do not').

Among the phrases we find for the first time in Shakespeare are:

to cudgel one's brains; a foregone conclusion; fair play; to breathe one's last; to bury unkindness; to lay odds; to wear your heart on your sleeve; to be sick of something; to paint from the life.

In these phrases Shakespeare seems to be extending the meaning of ordinary words; yet they bear the stamp of everyday proverbial speech. True, this may seem so to us because we in our turn have been using them familiarly since they were first printed in his works. Recent researches, however, have turned up many examples, in parish records, household accounts, and similar sources, of words and phrases once thought to be Shakespeare's creations.

The conclusion we reach, then, is that Shakespeare was not only a great innovator in that he created many words which appear for the first time in print; but that he was also receptive to dialect and colloquial usages which he incorporated into the literary language we still use today.

Puns and Plays on Words

All through his plays and poems Shakespeare shows that he took intense delight in words as things to play with. In the earliest plays there are a large number of puns and innuendoes (hidden meanings), especially in the comedies or in the lighter scenes of tragedies and histories. Even in the intensest moments of tragedy, a play on a word can startle us:

> Put out the light, and then put out the light,

says Othello, as he carries the candle into the chamber where he is to kill Desdemona.

True, in the earlier plays the punning word cannot carry such a depth of emotion, though Richard II, sorrowing in his cell at Pomfret Castle, can quibble on the meaning of 'time' as he hears the musicians playing carelessly:

> Ha, ha! keep time. How sour sweet music is
> When time is broke and no proportion kept!
> So is it in the music of men's lives.
> And here have I the daintiness of ear
> To check time broke in a disorder'd string;
> But, for the concord of my state and time,

Had not an ear to hear my true time broke.
I wasted time, and now doth time waste me . . .

RICHARD THE SECOND, 5, 5, 42-9

There are another twelve lines of this; no wonder Dr. Johnson was moved to say, 'A quibble was to him the fatal Cleopatra for which he lost the world.' This deliberate, extended punning is perhaps foreign to our own feelings, as it was to Johnson's.

The love of punning has a more natural outlet in the comedies, or in those lighter scenes where the company's clown is given employment. *Julius Caesar* begins with the witty cobbler offering to 'mend' the imperious tribune, Marullus, if he is 'out'. The clown Feste in *Twelfth Night* has an amusing passage of wit with Viola:

VIOLA: Save thee, friend, and thy music! Dost thou live by thy tabor?

CLOWN: No, sir, I live by the church.

VIOLA: Art thou a churchman?

CLOWN: No such matter, sir: I do live by the church; for I do live at my house, and my house doth stand by the church.

3, 1, 1-7

Some words are punned on by Shakespeare so often that it seems to become a habit with him. Among these are *crown, angel, hart—heart* and *deer—dear*. All these are usually doubled in meaning, and even trebled, as in this example from *Henry the Fifth* (though the third meaning, 'king's ceremonial head-dress', is only implied):

Indeed, the French may lay twenty French crowns to one they will beat us, for they bear them on their shoulders; but it is no English treason to cut French crowns, and to-morrow the King himself will be a clipper.

4, 1, 222-7

One of the bases of comedy, it is generally accepted, is this playing with language. Beatrice and Benedick in *Much Ado About Nothing* are perhaps the prime examples of this, and the

69

humour of Dogberry and Verges, in the same play, depends on their misuse of language. Long before Sheridan created Mrs. Malaprop they, with Mrs. Quickly and Bottom the Weaver, were ingeniously misapplying a 'nice derangement of epitaphs'.

In a more serious context, the play on words can add point to the expression of an idea. One of the themes constantly debated by Shakespeare is the effect of training and environment on the inborn nature of a man. In *The Tempest* this is epigrammatically and semi-punningly stated by Prospero in his description of Caliban as:

A devil, a born devil, on whose nature
Nurture can never stick . . .

4, 1, 188-9

It is the juxtaposition of the two similar sounds, 'nature' and 'nurture', that makes the lines memorable.

Not all of Shakespeare's puns are as seriously intended as this, nor are they all so innocent as the ones quoted from comic scenes. Many of his quibbles carry obscene hidden meanings which shocked the Victorians, those lovers of family readings; but we can be sure that Shakespeare's audience saw and enjoyed the bawdy jokes that he sprinkled through the comedies. Some of them are obvious; others require a specialised knowledge of Elizabethan low-life English. But in making them, Shakespeare was in no way remarkable in a franker age and a more robust society than the Victorian; his contemporaries are equally outspoken. And while he seems to have enjoyed punning and verbal gymnastics even more than his fellow playwrights did, he is certainly no bawdier than they are.

Latin or Anglo-Saxon?

Finally, let us try to answer the question: is Shakespeare's vocabulary predominantly Latinate or Anglo-Saxon? Some teachers of English style will assert that the best English is the simplest; that 'put off' is better than 'postpone', and that you do not ordinarily 'descend a declivity' but 'come down a hill'. They uphold Swift as an exponent of the simple style, and decry Dr. Johnson and Pope (especially in his translation of *The Iliad*) for the pomposity of their inflated language. Does it follow, then, that the best word is always the simplest basic Old English word?

Shakespeare's vocabulary gives no help to the doctrinaire upholders of Anglo-Saxon. It is, of course, true that many pathetic moments are expressed in the simplest words. There is not a single Latin word in the last speech of Lear; and the poignant words,

> Pray you undo this button. Thank you, sir.

> 5, 3, 309

could hardly be simpler.

On the other hand, there are many great moments that depend for their effect on specifically Latinate words. Macbeth's horror on seeing his bloody hands is expressed by:

> No; this my hand will rather
> The multitudinous seas incarnadine,
> Making the green one red.

> 2, 2, 61-3

The lovers of the simple may say here that 'incarnadine' is translated into telling monosyllables in the next line; but multitudinous' still remains.

Again, when Cleopatra dies we have the beautiful words:

> Now boast thee, death, in thy possession lies
> A lass unparallel'd.

> 5, 2, 313-4

Here the effect is made by the close connection of the simple monosyllable 'lass' with the long word 'unparallel'd', a dialect word with a classical one.

Shakespeare could summon up the right word for his purpose, from whatever source. Words were his complete servants, to be used in freedom and with authority. How fluent he was can only be conjectured. It was said of him that he never blotted a line; and he must have written pretty fast to produce so many plays in so comparatively brief a time. As his mastery grows, the words take on more and more power. For instance, in *The*

Winter's Tale (1610) he takes the noun 'climate' and bends it to his own syntactical purpose as a verb:

> The blessed gods
> Purge all infection from our air whilst you
> Do climate here!

5, 1, 168-70

In *The Tempest*, too, Alonso's guilt is brought home to him thus:

> . . . the thunder,
> That deep and dreadful organ-pipe, pronounc'd
> The name of Prosper; it did bass my trespass.

3, 3, 97-9

Here the word 'bass', usually a noun or adjective, is made to do Shakespeare's bidding in the guise of a verb. In each of these two examples the metaphor is compressed into one short word loaded with meanings and associations which are made all the more striking because Shakespeare wrenches the word from its usual function.

'Every vital development in language', says T. S. Eliot, 'is a development in feeling as well.' We can say, as Eliot says of Tourneur and Middleton, that Shakespeare exhibits 'that perpetual slight alteration of language, words perpetually juxta-posed in new and sudden combinations, meanings perpetually *eingeschachtelt* (inserted) into meanings, which evidences a very high development of the senses.'

It is because Shakespeare was so vital, so alive to the variety of life, so perpetually stimulated into thought, so deeply involved in the joys and sorrows of the teeming life around him, that his language is so virile, so flexible and so satisfying.

SHAKESPEARE'S VERSE

It may seem odd to us, who are used to seeing most of our modern plays written in prose, a few in verse, but hardly any in a mixture of the two, that Shakespeare uses so many different forms of expression in the same play; indeed, sometimes in the

Shakespeare's handwriting (?) from the Addition to the Play of *Sir Thomas More*—see pp. 55, 58.

        what Country by the nature of yor error
        shoold gyve you harber go yo^u to ffraunc or flanders
        to any Iarman province, spane or portigall
        nay any where that not adheres to Ingland
        why yo^u must needs be straingers, woold yo^u be pleasd
        to find a nation of such barbarous temper
        that breaking out in hiddious violence
        woold not afoord yo^u, an abode on earth
        whett their detested knyves against yor throtes
        spurne yo^u lyke doggs, and lyke as yf that god.
        owed not nor made not yo^u, nor that the elaments
        wer not all appropriat to yor Comforts.
        but Charterd unto them, what woold yo^u thinck
        to be thus usd, this is the straingers case
ALL   and this your mountainish inhumanyty

        fayth a saies trewe letts (vs) do as we may be doon by

LINCO weele be ruled by yo^u master moor yf youle stand our
        freind to procure our pardon

And so by continuance, and weakenesse of the braine
Into this frensie, which now possesseth him:
And if this be not true, take this from this.

    King Thinke you t'is so?
    Cor. How? so my Lord, I would very faine know
That thing that I haue saide t'is so, positiuely,
And it hath fallen out otherwise.
Nay, if circumstances leade me on,
Ile finde it out, if it were hid
As deepe as the centre of the earth.

    King. how should wee trie this same?
    Cor. Mary my good lord thus,
The Princes walke is here in the galery,
There let *Ofelia*, walke vntill hee comes:
Your selfe and I will stand close in the study,
There shall you heare the effect of all his hart,
And if it proue any otherwise then loue,
Then let my censure faile another time.

    King. see where hee comes poring vppon a booke.

           Enter Hamlet.

    Cor. Madame, will it please your grace
To leaue vs here?

    Que. With all my hart.   *exit.*
    Cor. And here *Ofelia*, reade you on this booke,
And walke aloofe, the King shal be vnseene.

    Ham. To be, or not to be, I there's the point,
To Die, to sleepe, is that all? I all:
No, to sleepe, to dreame, I mary there it goes,
For in that dreame of death, when wee awake,
And borne before an euerlasting Iudge,
From whence no passenger euer retur'nd,
The vndiscouered country, at whose sight
The happy smile, and the accursed damn'd.
But for this, the ioyfull hope of this,
Whol'd beare the scornes and flattery of the world,
Scorned by the right rich, the rich curssed of the poore?

                                  The

Part of the 'To be or not to be' speech from the First Quarto, 1603 (*above*), and from the Second Quarto, 1604 (*right*)—see p. 52.

We will bestow our selues; reade on this booke,
That show of such an exercise may cullour
Your lowlines; we are oft too blame in this,
Tis too much prou'd, that with deuotions visage
And pious action, we doe sugar ore
The deuill himselfe.

   King. O tis too true,
How smart a lash that speech doth giue my conscience,
The harlots cheeke beautied with plastring art,
Is not more ougly to the thing that helps it,
Then is my deede to my most painted word :
O heauy burthen.

         Enter Hamlet.
   Pol. I heare him comming, with-draw my Lord.
   Ham. To be, or not to be, that is the question,
Whether tis nobler in the minde to suffer
The slings and arrowes of outragious fortune,
Or to take Armes against a sea of troubles,
And by opposing, end them, to die to sleepe
No more, and by a sleepe, to say we end
The hart-ake, and the thousand naturall shocks
That flesh is heire to; tis a consumation
Deuoutly to be wisht to die to sleepe,
To sleepe, perchance to dreame, I there's the rub,
For in that sleepe of death what dreames may come
When we haue shuffled off this mortall coyle
Must giue vs pause, there's the respect
That makes calamitie of so long life :
For who would beare the whips and scornes of time,
Th'oppressors wrong, the proude mans contumely,
The pangs of despiz'd loue, the lawes delay,
The insolence of office, and the spurnes
That patient merrit of th'vnworthy takes,
When he himselfe might his quietas make
With a bare bodkin; who would fardels beare,
To grunt and sweat vnder a wearie life,
But that the dread of something after death,
The vndiscouer'd country, from whose borne

Picasso's Vision of Horror (Part of *Guernica*)—see pp. 110 et seqq

same scene we have blank verse, rhymed couplets, lyrics, and prose all mixed up together.

We will now take a look at the two main forms of language that he used, verse and prose, and see firstly how his mastery of verse developed as he grew older; and, secondly, try to answer the question why he used verse at some times and prose at others.

Blank Verse

Most of the verse is blank verse, a term usually applied to lines of ten alternately stressed syllables, without rhyme, sometimes called iambic pentameters (though this name properly applies only to Latin or Greek verse). This type of verse is very much used by English poets of all periods of our literature; two of our greatest poems (*Paradise Lost* by Milton, and *The Prelude* by Wordsworth) are written completely in blank verse; and the five-stressed, ten-syllabled line is very common in rhymed verse, ranging from the works of Chaucer to those of Dryden and Pope and nearly all eighteenth and nineteenth century poets.

The blank or unrhymed form of this ten-syllabled verse was introduced into English poetry by the Earl of Surrey shortly before Shakespeare was born; it is so suited to English ears that it was widely used in the early plays of the Elizabethan theatre, and by about 1590 it was established as the normal medium for drama. Writers such as George Peele, Robert Greene, and Christopher Marlowe were only the greatest of many who were using and perfecting this form of verse before Shakespeare himself began to write, but while he was in London as a young actor. To Marlowe is usually given the prize for blank verse before Shakespeare, and we can see in this passage from *Dr. Faustus* how majestic, yet how regular, Marlowe's 'mighty line' was:

Had I as many souls as there be stars,
I'd give them all for Mephistophilis.
By him I'll be great Emp'ror of the world,
And make a bridge thorough the moving air,

To pass the ocean with a band of men;
I'll join the hills that bind the Afric shore,
And make that country continent to Spain,
And both contributory to my crown:
The Emp'ror shall not live but by my leave,
Nor any potentate of Germany.

Scene 3, 104-16

Shakespeare at first wrote the same kind of regular verse:

Scarce can I speak, my choler is so great.
O, I could hew up rocks and fight with flint,
I am so angry at these abject terms;
And now, like Ajax Telamonius,
On sheep or oxen could I spend my fury.
I am far better born than is the King,
More like a king, more kingly in my thoughts;
But I must make fair weather yet a while,
Till Henry be more weak and I more strong.

2 HENRY THE SIXTH, 5, 1, 23-31

Each line but the fifth has exactly ten syllables; each line but
the fourth and fifth has a strongly stressed monosyllable to
end it; each line is end-stopped, that is, there is punctuation
at the end of the line because it is a grammatical unit, and the
voice tends to pause there in speaking the line. The rhythm is as
nearly regular as it is possible to get in English:

But I must make // fair weather yet a while,
Till Henry be more weak, // and I more strong.

In addition, each line has a slight pause called a caesura (though
it is not quite the same as the caesura in a line of Latin or Greek
verse) near the middle, usually after the second foot or the third
foot, that is, the fourth or sixth syllable. The only lines in the
passage above which have their pause elsewhere are the third
and fifth (where it comes in the middle of the third foot) and
the fourth, which has a long proper name of seven syllables.
This proportion is fairly general in Shakespeare's early verse.

Another aspect of this formal regularity is Shakespeare's use,
particularly in the early plays, of what is called 'patterned' blank

74

verse. Here all the sentences of a single passage may be carefully related in their structure, or a passage may be distributed among a number of characters. One of the most famous examples is the following piece from *Richard the Third* (1592):

Q. ELIZA.	What stay had I but Edward? and he's gone.
CHILDREN	What stay had we but Clarence? and he's gone.
DUCHESS	What stays had I but they? and they are gone.
Q. ELIZA.	Was never widow had so dear a loss.
CHILDREN	Were never orphans had so dear a loss.
DUCHESS	Was never mother had so dear a loss.

2, 2, 74-9

DEVELOPMENT OF SHAKESPEARE'S VERSE

Shakespeare thus was following Marlowe in his verse. But as he gained confidence and skill, and as his plays took on more stage movement and dramatic vigour, so his rhythm became less constrained. In the earlier plays, the characters tend to stand and deliver set-speeches in rhetorical terms; in the later plays they move about more, and converse in language whose rhythm is nearer to that of everyday life, the rhythm of prose.

The difference between the passage from *2 Henry the Sixth* (1590) and this passage from *Cymbeline* (1609) is quite obvious, so much so that it could well have been written by another poet:

O thou goddess,
Thou divine Nature, thou thyself thou blazon'st
In these two princely boys! They are as gentle
As zephyrs blowing below the violet,
Not wagging his sweet head; and yet as rough,
Their royal blood enchaf'd, as the rud'st wind
That by the top doth take the mountain pine
And make him stoop to th' vale. 'Tis wonder
That an invisible instinct should frame them
To royalty unlearn'd, honour untaught,
Civility not seen from other, valour
That wildly grows in them, but yields a crop
As if it had been sow'd.

4, 2, 170-82

75

Enjambment

The first thing we notice is that the line of verse is not the grammatical unit; the actor's voice does not, cannot, stop at the end of the line (except possibly in line 4). In other words, most lines run on in sense, and any pauses in the sense come in the middle of lines, or near the ends: lines 8 and 11 are good examples of this. This running on is called 'enjambment'.

Variation of Caesura

Secondly, the place of the caesura is more varied. In several lines the pause comes, as expected, at the end of the second or third foot. But in lines 2 and 4 it comes in the middle of the third foot; in line 9 it follows the seventh syllable; in line 11 it follows the eighth syllable; and line 8 is altogether odd, for though it has ten syllables it seems to lack a complete foot, the fourth, as if the actor here makes some movement or gesture which interrupts the flow of his thoughts.

Feminine Endings

More striking than the variation of caesura is the number of lines with extra syllables at the ends—so-called feminine endings, on an analogy with French poetry where the feminine form of the adjective usually adds an *e* to the masculine. In the passage from *Cymbeline* we have 'blazon'st', 'gentle', 'wonder', 'frame them', and 'valour', as well as 'goddess' in the first line. Analysis of the lines will show that in all cases (except the very irregular line 8 mentioned above) there are eleven syllables, and that the last, eleventh syllable is unaccented and falls outside or after the fifth foot: e.g.

In these / two prince / ly boys! / They are / as gent // le

Usually in Shakespeare the extra syllable is part of a two-syllabled or longer word; less often is it a monosyllable, as in line 9.

The effect of the feminine ending on the movement of the verse is remarkable. Read aloud to yourself a page of *Romeo and Juliet* or *Henry the Sixth*, and you will find it difficult to avoid chopping the speeches up into equal lines of seemingly equal weight in the progression of the argument. Here is a passage from *Romeo and Juliet* (1595):

> Many a morning hath he there been seen,
> With tears augmenting the fresh morning's dew,
> Adding to clouds more clouds with his deep sighs;
> But all so soon as the all-cheering sun
> 5 Should in the farthest east begin to draw
> The shady curtains from Aurora's bed,
> Away from light steals home my heavy son,
> And private in his chamber pens himself,
> Shuts up his windows, locks fair daylight out,
> 10 And makes himself an artificial night.

I, i, 129-38

Even where the sense requires the voice to run on, as in lines 4 and 5, the metre holds it back and encourages a slight pause at the ends of the lines. We may say that the increase in feminine endings combined with the increase in enjambment is the most striking characteristic of late Shakespearean verse.

Light and Weak Endings

There are, however, other variations from the strict metrical regularity of the early verse which are illustrated in this passage from *Coriolanus* (1607):

>   He that trusts to you,
> Where he should find you lions, finds you hares;
> Where foxes, geese; you are no surer, no,
> Than is the coal of fire upon the ice
> 5 Or hailstone in the sun. Your virtue is
> To make him worthy whose offence subdues him,
> And curse that justice did it. Who deserves greatness
> Deserves your hate; and your affections are
> A sick man's appetite, who desires most that
> 10 Which would increase his evil. He that depends
> Upon your favours swims with fins of lead,
> And hews down oaks with rushes.

I, i, 168-79

In lines 5 and 8 the last syllable, the tenth, should bear a stress; but the grammatically unimportant words 'is' and 'are' cannot do so, and the voice runs on to the next line from the 'light ending'. Lines of this type are very frequent in the last half dozen plays, but rare in the vast majority of Shakespeare's plays, those written before *Antony and Cleopatra* in 1607.

Weak endings should also be mentioned, though they can be classed with light endings. In these, a totally unimportant word such as 'and' comes last, as tenth syllable, in the line. For all practical purposes these are the same as light endings, increasing in number only at the end of Shakespeare's career, and having the effect of forcing the voice to run on to the next line and making it impossible for the hearer to conceive of the speeches as being written in verse. Indeed, this trick becomes frequent for the first time in *Antony and Cleopatra*, a play for which Shakespeare took whole pieces of someone else's prose and versified them with very little alteration.

Extra Syllables in Middle of Lines
The second variation shown by the *Coriolanus* passage is the trick of putting an extra syllable, like a feminine ending, at the end of a phrase or sentence but in the middle of a line of verse. Lines 7 and 10 show this clearly, with the words 'did it' and 'evil'. This also has the effect of breaking up the verse-flow, and becomes more frequent as Shakespeare grew older, being very rare in the early plays.

Speeches Beginning in Mid-line
Last comes a variation which it is impossible to illustrate in short quotations but which is obvious from a glance at the printed page. In the latest plays nearly every speech begins and ends in mid-line: whereas in the earliest plays the speeches all begin at the beginnings of lines, and, of course, end at the ends of lines. Again, this makes for the break-up of the verse form, with a consequent naturalness of rhythm, approximating ever more closely to that of prose as Shakespeare matures.

So remarkable are these variations from the normal Marlovian or early Shakespearean blank verse that it is possible, by statistical analysis of them, to date the plays in a chronological sequence. This process began two hundred years ago with the editor Malone (see p. 57); and one hundred years ago, at the end of the last century, both German and English scholars worked meticulously on the process and established a chronology which has not been seriously challenged since. Moreover, the authenticity of doubtful plays has been established or rejected by such tests. One does not, indeed, need to go into the mathematical calculations required. If you see *Henry the Eighth* produced, or listen to it on the radio, you will soon feel convinced, merely by the rhythm of the verse, that Shakespeare did not write very much of it, and that if he did write any of it, it was late in his career as a dramatist.

VARIATIONS IN THE USE OF RHYME

Apart from the many songs, there is a varying proportion of rhymed lines in the plays of Shakespeare. Some, such as *Julius Caesar*, have hardly any rhymed lines at all; while others vary: for example, *Richard the Second* has about one fifth, and *Love's Labour's Lost* as much as three-fifths. But the proportion of rhymed to blank lines is no guide to the date of a play in the Shakespeare chronology, though in the last plays there is almost none at all.

The 'Lyrical Period'

The plays with the most rhyme appear to have been written between the years 1593 and 1596. It was at this period also that Shakespeare was occupied in writing his long poems and possibly the *Sonnets*. There is thus a 'lyrical period', 1592-6, in which the following were written approximately at the dates given:

Venus and Adonis	1592
The Rape of Lucrece	1593
The Comedy of Errors	1593, 1 in 5 rhymed lines
Love's Labour's Lost	1594, 3 in 5 ,, ,,
Romeo and Juliet	1595, 1 in 5 ,, ,,
Richard the Second	1595, 1 in 5 ,, ,,
A Midsummer Night's Dream	1596, 2 in 5 ,, ,,
Sonnets	1593-96

It would seem that at this period Shakespeare was preoccupied with composing in rhyme, for he produced 199 stanzas of sesta rima (a quatrain followed by a couplet) in *Venus and Adonis*; 265 stanzas of rime royal (7 lines rhyming a. b. a. b. b. c. c.) and 154 sonnets of 14 lines each (though, to be accurate, one has 15!), as well as many hundreds of couplets and quatrains in the plays mentioned.

Two of the plays with an abundance of rhyme—*Love's Labour's Lost* and *A Midsummer Night's Dream*—were written primarily for elaborate court or private performance. The ornament of rhyme, which often offends our modern naturalistic ear, was a necessary ingredient in the fanciful story of these two plays; and again, rhyme would be more acceptable to the poetry-loving and verse-writing nobility than to the usual middle- or low-brow audience for whom most of the plays were written.

Other plays with much rhyme were written outside this 'lyrical period'. They are *Twelfth Night*, according to Dr. Hotson written for the Queen's Christmas festivities of 1600-1, and *All's Well That Ends Well*, about the date of which there is much controversy. In any case, half of it is in prose, and the rhymed verse falls mostly in the second category below (moralising rhymes).

Two plays which are usually considered to have been written during the 'lyrical period', yet which have comparatively little rhyme, are *The Taming of the Shrew* and *The Two Gentlemen of Verona*. Dr. Rowse in his biography puts these among the earliest of the plays, written before the truly lyrical ones; and there is no record of their performance at Court. They were popular successes. *The Comedy of Errors*, on the other hand, is very short and was written for performance in the Inns of Court, where, like *Love's Labour's Lost*, it would have a sophisticated audience who would appreciate the skill of the verse in this amalgam of two Latin plays by Plautus.

Apart from the plays of this period, then, where and why is rhyme used by Shakespeare?

Rhymed Endings to Scenes
First and most obvious, it is used to bring scenes to an end.

Usually the last two lines, and frequently the last four or even more, of a long blank verse scene will rhyme. This is clearly a device to end the scene in a tidy and definite way. It may possibly have had some practical use in giving a cue to the actors on the stage to leave it, and to those waiting for the next scene to come on, since there was no curtain on the apron stage to be conclusively drawn; or more likely, it was a sign to the audience that the scene had ended.

Moralising Rhymes

The second, more subtle, use of rhyme is in sententious hortatory or moralising speeches, in which the characters are, as it were, preaching to the others. Notable examples of this may be found in *King Lear*, when Kent is banished for opposing the King's will, and addresses the others in turn:

(TO THE KING)	Fare thee well, King. Sith thus thou wilt appear,
	Freedom lives hence, and banishment is here.
(TO CORDELIA)	The gods to their dear shelter take thee, maid,
	That justly think'st, and hast most rightly said!
(TO THE SISTERS)	And your large speeches may your deeds approve,
	That good effects may spring from words of love!
(TO THE REST)	Thus Kent, O princes, bids you all adieu;
	He'll shape his old course in a country new.

I, I, 180-7

Later in the same scene, the King of France, in accepting Cordelia as his wife, speaks eight lines of rhymed verse, to which Lear replies, equally formally, with four. After which Cordelia gives point to her battle of words with her sisters by means of rhyme, in which they reply to her:

CORDELIA: To your professed bosoms I commit him;
But yet, alas, stood I within his grace,
I would prefer him to a better place.
So, farewell to you both.
REGAN: Prescribe not us our duty.

GONERIL: Let your study
Be to content your lord, who hath receiv'd you
At fortune's alms. You have obedience scanted,
And well are worth the want that you have wanted.
CORDELIA: Time shall unfold what plighted cunning hides,
Who covers faults, at last with shame derides.

I, I, 272-81

These rhymes give sharpness of tone to the proverbial character of the thought.

A similar passage of rhymed verse occurs in *Othello*, when Brabantio has reluctantly agreed to the Duke's plea to let Othello have Desdemona. After the stirring eloquence of Othello's defence of his conduct and narration of how he wooed Desdemona, Desdemona's movingly simple speech about her 'divided duty', and Brabantio's heart-broken relinquishing of his only child, the Duke resorts to rhyme to clothe his advice to Brabantio, couched in proverbial 'sentences', and Brabantio replies in similar words and similar rhymed verse. Then the Duke, turning to the affairs of state, breaks into business-like prose, and the formalised moment of decision, one of the crises of the action, is over. This is also a striking example of the way in which Shakespeare can call upon a variety of language and of form within one scene in order to alter the pace and the tone of the action.

A third and more obviously structural use of rhyme hardly needs pointing out. It is used for such obvious interludes as the Marriage Masque in *The Tempest*, the epilogue in *Henry the Fifth*, and the speech of Time at the beginning of Act 4 of *The Winter's Tale*.

SHAKESPEARE'S PROSE

Shakespeare did not always write verse in the plays; nearly all of them contain some scenes, or parts of scenes, in prose. Some plays, indeed, have as much as three-quarters prose, and many have a half or a third.

Prose for Low Life

It is generally easy to see why Shakespeare chose verse for

some scenes and prose for others. In the history plays, *Henry the Fourth* and *Henry the Fifth*, where he presents not only the kings and nobles but also the common soldiers and the thieves and vagabonds, the political arguments take place in verse and the scenes of low life in prose. Falstaff, for instance, never speaks in verse, except when he is mocking the bombastic language of the stage in his comic imitation of a king (*1 Henry the Fourth* 2, *4*, 380); and while the Prince is with Falstaff or in the Boar's Head tavern he, too, speaks in prose. It is significant, though, that at the end of the very first prose scene in *1 Henry the Fourth*, when the Prince has dismissed his shallow companions, he speaks his soliloquy, his inmost thoughts, in verse.

> I know you all, and will awhile uphold
> The unyok'd humour of your idleness . . .

1, 2, 188-9

The true nature of a Prince is expressed in verse; and Shakespeare shows that Hal's loose behaviour is no more than a cloak which he can throw off at will, just as he throws off the loose prose to reveal the ordered regularity of the verse.

Similarly, in *Henry the Fifth*, when the king, prowling in disguise round the camp before Agincourt, comes upon the three sturdy soldiers, Bates, Court and Williams (4, *1*, 86) who 'inly ruminate The morning's danger', he joins them in their forebodings; the gloomy discussion of the rights and wrongs of the king's cause is carried on in prose, and culminates in a prose quarrel. But as soon as the king is alone again, he throws off the cloak of prose and meditates on the nature of Ceremony and Kingship in highly wrought rhetorical verse, representative of his true nature as a king.

A glance at the other prose scenes in *Henry the Fifth* further demonstrates the use of prose. Fluellen and the other captains squabble in prose; the Princess Katherine and her attendant Alice jabber in a sort of French prose; and the mocking French grandees jest against the foolish Dauphin in prose, though when they debate high politics they do it in verse. These are all comic scenes; they remove our interest from the hero king for a welcome diversion, and the contrast between these scenes and the serious, heroic verse scenes is all the more pointed by the change from prose to verse and back again.

Prose as a Contrast to Verse

Contrast is also the key to other uses of prose. In *King Lear*, for instance, the sub-plot of Gloucester and his sons mirrors on a lower plane the main story of Lear and his daughters, and is conducted largely in prose, while the main plot is in verse. When Lear goes mad, however, a good deal of his speech is in prose; but with his sanity comes back the verse, all the more beautiful by contrast with the troubled prose of his madness:

> You do me wrong to take me out o' th' grave.
> Thou art a soul in bliss; but I am bound
> Upon a wheel of fire, that mine own tears
> Do scald like molten lead.

4, 7, 45-8

Two other examples of this contrast are noteworthy. Many more could be cited, but these are typical:

In *Julius Caesar*, Brutus and Antony in turn address the Roman mob at Caesar's funeral. Brutus gives them 'reasons' why he killed Caesar, and in a perfectly modelled rhetorical speech convinces them by a show of logic, couched in clear, honest prose. But when Antony begins his speech, with feigned tears and disclaimers of oratorical skill, he is given verse to speak; and the emotional pitch is soon raised, by means of the verse, to frenzy. Reason is couched in prose, passion in verse.

The Winter's Tale follows the usual rule of verse for serious, prose for comic or less elevated scenes. After the first short scene of bantering small-talk, the royal scenes of the first three acts are spoken in verse; the first continuously used prose comes only with the entry of the shepherd and his clownish son (3, 3, 57). Autolycus, too, the jester, naturally speaks in prose; but Perdita and Florizel, though in disguise, shine as truly royal in their verse courtship, and even the old Shepherd is elevated for a time into poetical peerage with them, with Count Camillo and King Polixenes (4, 4). In the last Act, however, there are three scenes at the court of Leontes in Sicilia. The first and the third, as we might expect, are in verse, for they show the return of Perdita to her unknowing father, and the 'coming to life' of the apparent statue of Hermione. In between these, Shakespeare has to give us the news of the recognition by Leontes of his lost daughter, and so as not to detract from the majesty of the final reconciliation scene with the 'long dead' Hermione, he decides to narrate the meeting of the king and his daughter, and of the two kings, through the mouths of three court gentlemen. This scene would naturally fall into verse; but Shakespeare obviously wishes the final denouement, in the chapel where the 'statue' of Hermione awaits the unveiling, to be overwhelming in its impact. Hence he arranges the contrast, and gives it added point by ending the second scene with a few final jests from the Shepherd, Clown and Autolycus.

Apart from this general principle, prose is also used for letters and proclamations, as for the indictment of Hermione (3,2). Such uses are obvious and need no illustration here.

We may sum up, therefore, by saying that Shakespeare used prose

(a) for scenes of low, as opposed to high life.
(b) as a dramatic contrast with verse, in scenes (or acts) where a change of tone is needed.

Shakespeare's 'Prose Period'

It so happens that the middle plays of Shakespeare's career nearly all have a great deal of prose. The proportions are:

1597	*1 Henry the Fourth*	47 per cent	
1598	*2 Henry the Fourth*	53 "	"
1599	*Henry the Fifth*	42 "	"
1598	*The Merry Wives of Windsor*	88 "	"
1599	*Much Ado About Nothing*	75 "	"
1600	*As You Like It*	57 "	"
1600	*Twelfth Night*	64 "	"

The obvious reason for the general preponderance of prose in these plays is that they are full of comic scenes. Falstaff is prominent in the first two historical plays, and *The Merry Wives of Windsor* is almost entirely given up to his misfortunes. In *Henry the Fifth*, as we have seen, the king is not the sole centre of interest. In the other three comedies, too, there is an alternation of serious and not so serious scenes, and while these comedies may be called 'romantic', they are not 'lyrical' in the same way as *A Midsummer Night's Dream* is, with its fairies and its scenes of love in the enchanted woods.

The comedy of this 'period' is not so fantastic; its characters speak in the accents of ordinary human beings, and convince us of the reality of their existence. Beatrice and Benedick live and breathe; by comparison, Hermia and Helena in *A Midsummer Night's Dream* are cardboard figures, beautifully dressed but not convincing as people.

Indeed, one editor, J. Dover Wilson, finds in *Much Ado About Nothing* what he calls 'verse fossils', that is, pieces of verse embedded in the prose, like ammonites in limestone. He suggests that Shakespeare took an earlier verse play about Claudio and Hero, their wooing and quarrel, and her 'miraculous' restoration to life, and re-wrote much of it in prose. Certainly it is Beatrice and Benedick who capture our interest: their predicament derives from their characters, and most of their war of wits is carried on in prose; whereas Claudio and Hero recede into the background of our interest, though nominally their story constitutes the main plot.

Shakespeare is at this time creating his characters by means of prose rather than verse, and it is generally agreed that in learning to give Falstaff and Fluellen life in dramatic prose— that is, words and phrases which reveal their characters—he was preparing himself for the dramatic verse out of which he later created Hamlet and Othello, Antony and Coriolanus. In his earlier plays, *Love's Labour's Lost, Romeo and Juliet,* and *Richard the Second,* for instance, the verse was static and decorative. In the later tragedies it is dynamic; the characters speak verse and use images appropriate both to their natures and to the situations they are enmeshed in. The 'prose period' comes in between.

M. Crane: *Shakespeare's Prose* (Phoenix PB, Chicago, 1963).

B. Ifor Evans: *The Language of Shakespeare's Plays* (Methuen PB, 1965).

G. S. Gordon: *Shakespeare's English* (S.P.E. Tract xxix, 1928).

Hilda M. Hulme: *Explorations in Shakespeare's Language* (Longmans Green, 1962).

M. Joseph: *Shakespeare's Use of the Arts of Language* (Hafner PB, 1966).

M. Mahood: *Shakespeare's Wordplay* (Methuen PB, 1968).

Shakespeare Survey, Vol. 7, is concerned with Shakespeare's language.

5

Shakespeare's Imagery

Of recent years, the study of Shakespeare has become increasingly involved in the actual words he wrote. Plays, scenes, lines and even words are subjected to close analysis; often the interpretation of a whole scene can depend on the meaning the critic finds in a single word. This kind of study makes it all the more important—as we have seen in Chapter 3—to establish exactly what Shakespeare said.

It is also necessary to grasp the importance now given to Shakespeare's similes and metaphors, collectively called imagery. Here we want first to discuss what imagery is, and then show how Shakespeare's imagery changed its nature as he developed as a poet, until in the greatest plays it is as important as the characters themselves, whose essential being is often most clearly revealed in the images the poet gives them to utter.

THE NATURE OF IMAGERY

The essence of poetry is imagery: the illumination of thought by a comparison between two basically dissimilar objects or ideas, which are suddenly seen to be in some way related, in a flash of imaginative insight. When Burns writes,

> My love is like a red red rose
> That's newly sprung in June,

he is isolating some of the qualities of the rose (for instance, its beauty, its scent, its colour, its freshness) and associating these, and only these, with similar qualities in his love; ignoring other qualities which are not present in his imagination at the same time (his love's eight stone, or her pimples, and the rose's thorns and its woody stem). The result is that we realise, instantaneously, that *his feeling* for his love is much the same as *our feeling* for a rose. Such a statement is not a logical or factual one, for a girl is not at all like a rose really.

Similes such as this, and their more compressed counterparts, metaphors, are our best means of experiencing and evaluating the power and range of a poet's imagination.

Hence we would expect a young poet's imagery to be very different from that of his mature years. As the man grows older, so his experience of life widens and deepens; the images that present themselves to his imagination at the age of twenty-five will show marked dissimilarity with those of a man of fifty.

In Shakespeare's case, these dissimilarities can be well illustrated by two examples, one from what may be his first play, and one from his last:

> And as the butcher takes away the calf,
> And binds the wretch, and beats it when it strays,
> Bearing it to the bloody slaughter-house,
> Even so, remorseless, have they borne him hence;
> And as the dam runs lowing up and down,
> Looking the way her harmless young one went,
> And can do nought but wail her darling's loss,
> Even so myself bewails good Gloucester's case
> With sad unhelpful tears, and with dimm'd eyes
> Look after him, and cannot do him good,
> So mighty are his vowed enemies.
>
> 2 HENRY THE SIXTH, 3, *1*, 210-20

> The government I cast upon my brother
> And to my state grew stranger, being transported
> And rapt in secret studies. Thy false uncle
> ....
> Being once perfected how to grant suits,
> How to deny them, who t'advance, and who
> To trash for over-topping, new created
> The creatures that were mine, I say, or chang'd 'em,
> Or else new form'd 'em; having both the key
> Of officer and office, set all hearts i' th' state
> To what tune pleas'd his ear; that now he was

> The ivy which had hid my princely trunk
> And suck'd my verdure out on't.

THE TEMPEST, I, 2, 75-87

In the first passage one idea is carried through eleven lines; while in the second there are at least seven different metaphors (cast, transported, trash for overtopping, created, key—in two senses —tune, ivy). This is the striking thing to learn about the development of Shakespeare's imagery; the first piece, with its long image developed over eleven lines, is characteristic of his early work, and the second, with its mixture of metaphors, is a good example of his later style. Consequently, if you can see that in a given passage the images are piled one on another, you will be confident that the passage is a fairly late one.

Other examples of the contrast between early and late imagery can be seen in some of the passages quoted in Chapter 4. The passage from *Coriolanus* (p. 77) has four different sets of images (animals, coals of fire on ice, a sick man's appetite, swimming with fins of lead); that from *Cymbeline* (p. 75) has at least three in thirteen lines; while the ten lines from *Romeo and Juliet* (p. 77) pursue one idea only, and the *Richard the Second* passage (p. 68) also confines itself to one extended metaphor (though here there is a double meaning in the word *time*).

With this basic difference firmly fixed in our minds, let us go into a little more detail.

IMAGERY IN THE EARLY PLAYS

Not all the images in the early plays are long elaborations continuing for a dozen lines, though many of them are. Sometimes Shakespeare confines himself to two or three lines, as in the words spoken by Romeo as he sees the body of Juliet in the tomb of the Capulets:

> Thou art not conquer'd; beauty's ensign yet
> Is crimson in thy lips and in thy cheeks,
> And death's pale flag is not advanced there.

ROMEO AND JULIET, 5, 3, 94-6

Sometimes, too, he adds one short image to another, often in single complete lines of verse, or in two or three complete lines joined together; as if his mind is working in lines of verse and single images each complete in itself. There is in fact a tendency to use the images merely as ornaments to the thought; when someone has a statement to make he usually decorates it—sometimes with a long image, but often with a succession of images which may or may not be related to each other:

> Henry my lord is cold in great affairs,
> Too full of foolish pity; and Gloucester's show
> Beguiles him as the mournful crocodile
> With sorrow snares relenting passengers;
> Or as the snake, roll'd in a flow'ring bank,
> With shining checker'd slough, doth sting a child
> That for the beauty thinks it excellent.

2 HENRY THE SIXTH, 3, 1, 224-30

It is quite obvious that Shakespeare is here imitating rhetorical models, trying to achieve symmetry by balancing one word or one idea against another, though dramatically this parallelism is by no means necessary, and is indeed often harmful, to the differentiation of characters. As we previously said, in the early plays the persons stand around and deliver set speeches like orators addressing an audience. Again, we cannot tell merely from the style of the speeches who are the speakers, for they all strive after this symmetry of phrase or idea, and their images are not all characteristic of their different natures.

We are never able to forget in these early plays that rhetoric was one of the main subjects taught in the schools of the time, and of course at the very good Grammar School in Stratford. The student had to learn all the rhetorical devices in the book, just as we today learn the different sorts of conditional clauses in Latin, or the various uses of the subjunctive in French.

Thus we may say that dramatically the images of the early plays are unnecessary; we could omit them, for the most part, without harming either the story or our conception of the characters. They are rhetorical ornaments—figures of speech only and literally. Just as the young Shakespeare seemed, in his 'lyrical period', to enjoy making smooth verses and perfect rhymes, so he took delight in imagery for its own sake. Just as he copied the blank verse of Marlowe, so he drew on a common literary stock of images.

You may have wondered, when you read the passage last quoted, where Shakespeare had seen a crocodile snaring compassionate travellers by its tears, or even how many times he had seen a snake sting a child who picked up its discarded skin. The answer is that he was merely borrowing the conventional pictures that all Elizabethan poets and playwrights used, and which recur all over the writings of the time. The main source of these common images, largely drawn from nature, though often mythological or legendary nature, like the crocodile's tears, was Lyly's *Euphues* (see p. 16). It is the style of this book that gives us the word *euphuistic*, and though Shakespeare in his early career (and sometimes in the later plays, too, for special effects) himself writes in this rather ridiculous manner, he makes Falstaff mock it when imitating the King in the Boar's Head tavern in *1 Henry the Fourth*:

> ... for though the camomile, the more it is trodden on the faster it grows, yet youth, the more it is wasted the sooner it wears. ... There is a thing, Harry, which thou hast often heard of, and it is known to many in our land by the name of pitch. This pitch, as ancient writers do report, doth defile; so doth the company thou keepest ...

2, 4, 389-400

We may sum up by saying that the early images were rhetorical, conventional, euphuistic, and by no means dramatic; that is to say, they were not appropriate either to the characters who uttered them or to the situation on the stage.

SHAKESPEARE'S MATURE IMAGERY

If the essence of poetry is imagery, and the mature Shakespeare was a supreme poet, it is clear that a few pages of this book cannot go very far in revealing the secrets of his poetry; but here follows an attempt to define the main features of his later imagery, first in isolation and then in its dramatic context.

The most striking feature is the 'mixture of metaphors'. The most famous example of this occurs in *Antony and Cleopatra*, where the defeated Antony is bewailing the fickleness of his followers who have deserted to Caesar:

> All come to this? The hearts
> That spaniel'd me at heels, to whom I gave
> Their wishes, do discandy, melt their sweets
> On blossoming Caesar; and this pine is bark'd
> That overtopp'd them all.

4, 12, 20-4

To follow the thought through these five lines requires considerable mental agility. Looked at in cold logic, how can hearts be spaniels, and at the same time discandy and melt their sweets; and what thanks would the blossoming Caesar give for being covered in melting sugar? And when you have worked that out, how can they all be overtopped by a barked pine tree? This is the sort of 'wildness' (as Milton reminds us in *L'Allegro*) we hear when we listen to

> . . . sweetest Shakespeare, Fancy's child,
> Warble his native wood-notes wild . . .

It is this mixture of metaphors that underlay the general opinion of the eighteenth century, expressed as early as 1681 when the Poet Laureate, Nahum Tate, in his dedication of *King Lear* referred to the play as 'a Heap of Jewels, unstrung and unpolisht'. Tate, in recasting the whole play, 'used less Quaintness of Expression', and thought he was improving on Shakespeare.

The early editors, indeed, often emended what to our modern ears sounds eloquent and significant. We do not find any difficulty when Macbeth 'hath murder'd sleep'. Yet Steevens (1793) preferred a more logical statement: 'Macbeth hath murder'd a sleeper'. Logical this may be, but it has not a tenth of the force of the original 'unpolish jewel'.

Again, when Hamlet takes 'arms against a sea of troubles', we see in a flash that Hamlet's case is as hopeless as this act would be; yet various editors would have him take arms against 'assay' or even 'a siege' of troubles. It is not, as Christopher Ricks points out in his book *Milton's Grand Style*, that mixed metaphors do not matter. They are often ludicrous in the hands of ordinary writers, and should be avoided by anyone wishing to make a plain statement of fact or argument or exposition. But in a poet's hands the mixed metaphor is a source of power. Every metaphor, or image, is an illogical statement, not to be taken literally; we can therefore see each one as a source of new meaning. When two such metaphors are 'mixed', they interact, and the x of one seems to reinforce and multiply the x of the other, resulting in not $2x$ but x^2; and Shakespeare leads us on to x^3, x^4, x^n.

Shelley said, 'When my brain gets heated with thought, it soon boils, and throws off images and words faster than I can skim them off'. This feature of the creative process must have been prominent in the case of Shakespeare, too, and his practised pen could reduce the profusion of images to an imaginative order where logic had no place.

DRAMATIC APPROPRIATENESS

We said of the earlier imagery that it was merely decorative, like the verse, and like many other rhetorical devices, such as alliteration and amplification, and that it had no dramatic function; that the characters who spoke the lines were rarely expressing their own natures in their language. Of the images in the later plays, especially of the great tragedies, this is not true. Here the imagery has become one of the means—some critics would say the chief means—by which we know the essential nature of the characters and also of the play as a whole.

Imagery as a revelation of character

The most striking example of this may be found in *Othello*. The essence of this play is a conflict between the noble, passionate, exotic Othello and the cynical, calculating, worldly Iago. It is not only by their actions and in their sentiments that these two opponents are made real to us; their languages, and above all their images, are sharply contrasted.

Most noticeable is the profusion of imagery in Othello's

speech. He utters far more images, mostly metaphors, than Iago, and these metaphors arise directly and spontaneously from his personal senses and emotions. He speaks in an exaggerated way:

> O my soul's joy!
> If after every tempest come such calms,
> May the winds blow till they have waken'd death . . .
>
> <div align="right">2, <i>1</i>, 182-4</div>

> Blow me about in winds, roast me in sulphur,
> Wash me in steep-down gulfs of liquid fire.
>
> 5, 2, 282-3

Again, Othello's references to exotic places and peoples are characteristic of an 'extravagant and wheeling stranger', as he is contemptuously called. He mentions Arabian trees, antres vast and deserts idle, the Pontic sea, the ice-brook that tempers the sword of Spain, the anthropophagi and men whose heads do grow beneath their shoulders. And when he speaks of war, his element and his 'occupation', he thinks of its pride, pomp and circumstance.

By contrast, Iago talks of 'the trade of war'; his view of the world is a mercenary one, '—put money in thy purse'. Love he sees only as a 'raging motion' and a 'carnal sting'. Above all, his language (often prose, which Othello speaks only after his personal nobility is destroyed) is full of references to the baser activities of despised animals: asses, spiders, cats, dogs, goats and monkeys. He tends to use similes, which are more calculated and reasoned out than metaphors.

But most significant of all is the way in which the cynical bestiality of Iago infects the nobility of Othello during the critical scene (3, 3) when the first poison is poured into Othello's mind. It is a wonderful stroke of Shakespeare's to herald this change from an ordered serenity to a bestial corruption by the words:

> Excellent wretch! Perdition catch my soul
> But I do love thee; and when I love thee not
> Chaos is come again.
>
> <div align="right">3, <i>3</i>, 91-3</div>

From this moment, Othello, like Iago, begins to use bestial images. Iago does not need to work on him long before he is saying: 'Exchange me for a goat' (3, *3*, 184) and 'I had rather be a toad' (3, *3*, 274). This is the beginning of the corruption of his integrity; he renounces the plumed troops, and opens his mind to goats, monkeys and wolves. There could be no clearer indication of Shakespeare's skill in the use of imagery as a delineator of character.

IMAGERY OF A WHOLE PLAY

Certain kinds of image are predominant in each of the great tragedies. In *Hamlet* there is a perpetual reference to disease, poison, decay and rottenness: the Ghost, poisoned by a 'leperous distilment'; Hamlet himself, who sees the world as a 'foul and pestilent congregation of vapours'; Claudius, a 'mildew'd ear, Blasting his wholesome brother'; Denmark, a state in which 'something is rotten'; the whole world 'an unweeded garden That grows to seed'; Ophelia is called a 'breeder of sinners'; and Polonius will finally go, like any king, 'a progress through the guts of a beggar'. Examples of this preoccupation with disease and mortality abound; so much so that the standard picture of Hamlet, reproduced in statues and on postage stamps, is of a lean figure in black holding a skull in his hands, about to throw it into the grave—'And smelt so? Pah!'

In *King Lear* the commonest images are those of animals of prey; while storm and tempest sound throughout the play, both externally and in the mad king's mind. The play may be seen to express, among other things, a revulsion from mankind; and this is epitomised in the frequent comparison of the two sisters, Regan and Goneril, to fierce and cruel animals: the kite, the wolf, the serpent, the dog, the tiger and the vulture. Indeed, unless we take account of the imagery in this, or any other play of Shakespeare's, we cannot apprehend its inner meaning. It is this, rather than the fact that much of the plays are written in verse, that qualifies them to be called Poetic Drama.

Space does not permit us to explore in detail the other main image themes, especially the atmosphere of fear and darkness in

Macbeth, for instance. But we cannot end without closer reference to the supreme example of the domination of a whole play by one image: *The Tempest.* The title itself gives us the first clue to the workings of Shakespeare's mind, and the opening scene is not merely a bit of misplaced masque, or pantomime, performed to catch the attention of the audience, but an epitome of the symbolism of the play. In common with *The Winter's Tale, Cymbeline* and perhaps *Pericles,* which also has a highly symbolic tempest, this play is a long way from being a realistic picture of the world as it is. On Prospero's island, that world in little, we are never out of sound of the sea, still reverberating from the storm. Page after page has a reference to the winds and waves; and the heavenly music which Prospero eventually conjures up before he breaks his magic staff is a resolution of the discords of the earthly elements. Tempest is chaos, horror, destruction; music (and even Caliban can hear it when he is not beset with devils) is order, love, creation. We may not go as far as Professor Wilson Knight, but we must refer to his view, fascinatingly expounded through a series of books including *The Shakespearean Tempest,* that in the last masterpieces of Shakespeare 'the poetic image tends not only to blend with, but actually to become the plot'. Perhaps, for our purposes, nothing so strongly suggests the importance of the imagery as the fact that it has led us into the content of the next chapter about the 'meaning' of the plays.

READING LIST

W. H. Clemen: *The Development of Shakespeare's Imagery* (Methuen PB, 1966).
C. Spurgeon: *Shakespeare's Imagery* (Cambridge PB, 1965).
G. W. Knight: *The Shakespearean Tempest* (Methuen, 1932).
K. Muir: 'Shakespeare's Imagery—Then and Now', *Shakespeare Survey,* Vol. 18 (Cambridge).

6

Shakespeare's Moral Vision

One of the reasons for Shakespeare's greatness is the immense range of his work, from lightest comedy, as in *Twelfth Night*, to profoundest tragedy, as in *King Lear*. In reading a comedy we may well be quite unaware of the darker side of his genius; each play must first be judged on its own, just as we enjoy it on its own, without reference to the others in all their variety.

Nevertheless, it is helpful to the understanding of Shakespeare to see how each play is related to the others. There must be some central line through Shakespeare's philosophy, his view of life, his moral vision, that allows us to place each play either to one side of it or the other. After all, he was a mature man of twenty-six when he began to write; and we expect a great writer, such as Milton or Wordsworth, or Graham Greene or William Golding in our own day, to take up some attitude towards life, to commit himself to a point of view from which he looks at the human condition. To Milton, for instance, everything that had ever happened, before and after Eve's eating of the apple, was ordained by a wise and loving, but stern, God; and, in his *Paradise Lost*, he tried to show us the rightness of this view and to 'justify the ways of God to men'.

What was Shakespeare's moral vision? How did he see life? We can only guess at this, deducing from the many-coloured speeches of his thirty-seven plays some one central theme. He does not tell us, as Milton did at the very beginning of his poem, what his philosophy was; a play is not primarily a sermon or a propaganda handout—though some modern dramatists, from Shaw to Wesker, seem to think so. There will be differences of opinion about Shakespeare's views; and all that this short chapter does is to indicate one moral framework which may provide something to argue against as you come to know the plays in greater detail. In other words, we will say what we feel these plays are about; but we do not expect agreement at all points, for each play is far more subtly complex than will appear from our treatment of it in this chapter.

THE ELIZABETHAN PATTERN

Shakespeare's personal view of life was based on the generally held views of the men of his time. Elizabethan thinkers had a clear, well-defined plan of what we call the Universe, and they called the World; perhaps the word Cosmos is the best one for us to use here. They did not know (as we know today) that the Cosmos was infinite in its size, that it was expanding at unimaginable speed, and that light took millions of years to reach us from remote galaxies. Their Cosmos was like a beautiful, intricate machine, such as an ingenious clockmaker might construct, where each thing or person had its place, and was perfectly adapted to its function in that place, if only it would be content to obey the rule of law, which, according to Richard Hooker's *Laws of Ecclesiastical Polity* (1594), was:

> that which doth assign unto each thing the kind, that which doth moderate the force and power, that which doth appoint the form and measure of working.

God had created the Cosmos perfect; he had imposed order on chaos; the 'wondrous architecture', as Marlowe called it, was not the result of accident; the events of history were not blindly caused, but followed each other in a providential order. Everyone (except perhaps the followers of Machiavelli) believed in this rule of law, and in the order which God had ordained; sermons embodying the teaching of it were read on certain appointed Sundays of the year, so that all people might know it. One such Homily published in 1547, entitled *An Exhortation concerning Good Order and Obedience to Rulers and Magistrates,* actually used these words:

Almighty God hath created and appointed all things, in heaven, earth and waters, in a most excellent and perfect order. In heaven he hath appointed distinct orders and states of archangels and angels. In the earth he hath assigned kings, princes, with other governors under them, all in good and necessary order. The water above is kept and raineth down in due time and season. The sun, moon, stars, rainbow, thunder, lightning, clouds, and all birds of the air do keep their order. . . . [So with plants, animals, seasons, fishes, seas.] And man himself also hath all his parts both within and without, as soul, heart, mind, memory, understanding, reason, speech . . . in a profitable, necessary and pleasant order. Every degree of people in their vocation, calling and office hath appointed to them their duty and order. Some are in high degree, some in low . . . and every one have need of other, so that in all things is to be lauded and praised the goodly order of God, without the which no house, no city, no commonwealth can continue and endure.

Elizabethan thinkers were greatly preoccupied with the concept of order, obedience to the law; and this law they thought of as being subdivided into Natural Law, Celestial Law, Rational Law, Divine Law and Human Law. It was obedience to Human Law that bound the state (commonwealth, as they called it) together. The other forms of law operated in their different spheres, but each was essential to the perfect working of the cosmic machine; each was dependent on the others for its right functioning. Upset the Human Law by killing the king (also a crime against the Divine Law), and the Celestial Law, and the other laws too, are also upset; when Duncan is murdered, in *Macbeth*, the sun goes into eclipse, and Duncan's horses eat each other—a transgression against the Natural Law. As Shakespeare says in *Julius Caesar*:

When beggars die there are no comets seen:
The heavens themselves blaze forth the death of princes.

2, 2, 30-1

Thus each part of the Cosmos had a natural function, according to its *kind*, another way of saying its *nature*; and on its proper working, or obedience to the Law, was based its relationship with every other part.

How did these relationships work? Obviously there must be leaders and followers, those who commanded and those who obeyed, in varying degrees of importance. In other words, hierarchies were established, like the chain of command in an army from General down to Private (or the pecking order in a hen run). The word 'Chain' actually appears in philosophical literature of the Elizabethan age: a phrase later used was 'The Great Chain of Being'. At the lowest level were the stones, which had only *being*; then came plants, which were superior to stones because they had both *being* and *growth*; above them were animals, which enjoyed *sense* as well as *being* and *growth*; superior to animals was Man, who added the power of *reason* to the former qualities. This was the earthly hierarchy; but above man were the Angels (themselves in nine ranks) whose nature, or kind, was pure *reason*, man's highest quality; and at the top, unrealisable by mere sublunar creatures, was God, whose nature was pure *actuality*.

Again, within man himself was a hierarchy of corporal and spiritual parts. The body has three centres: the brain, at the top, was obviously the seat of reason; the heart, lower, was the seat of sensation, or emotion; and the liver, at the lowest level, was the seat of man's animal being. Look at the first scene of *Twelfth Night* to see a reference to this in Orsino's praise of his idolised Olivia. To us, the liver is the seat of the hangover; not so to Shakespeare.

Further, in the brain of man, too, there was another hierarchy, or chain of being: at the top, the understanding (dependent on pure reason); and beneath it the memory, the fancy (or imagination), the common-sense and the five senses, or five wits.

And just as the Cosmos moved in harmony so long as Law was obeyed, so man's mind remained sane only so long as no one part of it rebelled against the others, but continued content in its proper function. As Wilson said, in his *Art of Rhetoric* (1553):

> Temperance is a measuring of affections according to the will of reason, and a subduing of lust unto the square of honesty.

But temperance, or self-control, was not an automatic or easy state to achieve; Shakespeare's tragic heroes, as we shall see later, were incapable of achieving it—hence their downfall, and with them the ruin of many innocent persons and often of the commonwealth itself.

It is important to grasp this if we are to understand how Shakespeare's mind, and his audience's minds, worked. Our society and our philosophy are not tied to the idea of hierarchies, divinely ordained and never to be overthrown, as the Elizabethans' were. Besides, subsequent history has seen the downfall of so many kings, the upsetting of so many orders, that we have come to think of these unnatural, *unkind* acts as necessary for progress, a concept that we still believe salutary, despite much evidence to the contrary. But to Shakespeare's contemporaries, social order was the supreme political good; it was based on justice, respect for Law, in which Divine providence and human temperance worked together for the good of all. The king was not just a figurehead, but God's chosen instrument, almost God himself—hedged by Divinity, as Claudius said; and below him all the others were established in their various degrees. As Sir John Elyot said in *The Governor* (1531), the political whole was 'disposed by the order of equity, and governed by the rule and moderation of reason'.

Thus the Elizabethans saw a pattern in the world, not just a confused jumble of conflicting objects. They took delight in elaborating the pattern, and used their ingenuity to draw what they called 'correspondences' between one part of the pattern and the others. For instance, man was a microcosm (a little world) which reflected and was influenced by a macrocosm (or large world). Each link in the Chain of Being had its leader, or primacy, as they called it. (We still call the Archbishop of Canterbury the Primate of All England.) The primacy in stones (the lowest link in the chain) was the diamond; the primacy in metals was gold; other primacies were the eagle, the lion and the dolphin, and we still keep them alive, though unknowingly, by giving gold and diamond rings as engagement tokens, and by putting the eagle, not the sparrow, and the lion, not the rabbit, on our national flags. To Shakespeare's audience, the king was as the sun to the stars; Louis XIV called himself *Le Roi Soleil* in the next century, and even to us in the twentieth, the kingly crown is unthinkable except in gold. So when Shakespeare thinks of the king, he quite naturally thinks also of gold and of the sun; many are the references to these other primacies in speeches about kings; and when the bleeding Sergeant in *Macbeth* wants to convey the impossibility of overcoming the valour of Macbeth and Banquo, he says they were dismayed as much as eagles would be by sparrows or as lions by hares.

Another pattern could be seen in the division of the universe into two; the sublunar part, which was subject to time and constituted of the four elements, in their hierarchical order of earth, water, fire and air; and the celestial part, with its various planetary spheres, which was eternal and above the lunar sphere. Creation was divided into two corresponding parts, animal and angelic. The bodily or corporeal part of man himself depended for health on a proper balance, or obedience to natural law, of the four humours, or bodily fluids, which again were formed of and corresponded to the four elements.

But the cosmic pattern was not only an intricate one; it was a moving one, displaying the shifting order of a ceremonial dance. Sir John Davies, a minor poet, wrote in 1596 in a poem called *Orchestra,* which means dancing-place in Greek:

> Kind nature first doth cause all things to love;
> Love makes them dance and in just order move.

The key to the whole pattern, therefore, was firstly Law, and secondly Love. Love made the whole pattern dance 'in just order'. It was God's love which had originally created the Cosmos out of Chaos; it was human love, particularly in its most spiritual forms, which produced sense and order out of man's faculties. Here two other great ideas which governed European thought came in. The first is the ideal of Courtly Love, which found its most famous expression in the mediaeval French poem, *The Romance of the Rose,* which Chaucer translated and which had an immense influence on the chivalric society of the centuries before Shakespeare. The second is the idea of neo-Platonism, a mystical belief, popularised by the philosophers of renaissance Florence and at the heart of Dante's *Divine Comedy*, that through love's various stages man could achieve union with the Divine. One of the best-known descriptions of the power of love comes in Hoby's translation (1561) of an Italian book, *The Courtier*:

> Thou with agreement bringest the elements in one, stirrest nature to bring forth. . . . Thou bringest severed matters into one, to the imperfect givest perfection, to the unlike likeness, to enmity amity, to the earth fruits, to the sea calmness, to the heaven lively light. Thou art the father of the true pleasures, of grace, peace, lowliness and goodwill, enemy to rude wildness and sluggishness; to be short, the beginning and end of all goodness.

Through love, man submitted to the cosmic pattern. A favourite text of Elizabethan preachers came from Paul's *Epistle to the Romans*:

> Render therefore to all their dues: tribute to whom tribute is due; custom to whom custom; fear to whom fear; honour to whom honour.

Richard Hooker wrote:

> Obedience of creatures unto the Law of Nature is the stay of the whole world.

This was particularly important to man, because his position in the Chain of Being was difficult to maintain. His duty was to strive for the higher nature of the angels above him against the appetites of his bestial lower nature. He was placed between the higher realms of spiritual grace and the lower realm of physical gratification of the senses, between right reason and destructive passion, and it was his endless task to establish a harmony between these opposites that could only be a precarious one at its best. As Philemon Holland wrote in his translation (1603) of Plutarch's *Morals*:

> One part [of the soul of men] is more spiritual, intelligible and

104

reasonable, which ought of right and according to nature to have the sovereignty and command in man; the other is brutish, sensual, erroneous and disorderly of itself, requiring the direction and guidance of another [i.e. part of the soul].

The essence of the human predicament was that a man had freedom to decide whether to accept or reject this loving right-relationship. All drama is based on conflict, and it is this idea of choosing one line of action, rather than another, that constitutes the conflict in Shakespeare's plays. Here, particularly in the tragedies, the hero's moment of choice is often the springboard of the whole action. Will he choose that line of action which accords with law and obedience to the call of love, or will he side with his baser nature and reject the right-relationship? Macbeth is a clear case of this; so is Othello.

According to Christian teaching, there had already been a wrong choice, based on disobedience and pride, as Milton later showed in Book IX of *Paradise Lost*, when Adam and Eve deliberately flouted God's command not to eat of the Tree of Knowledge. As a result of their fall from grace, which all their descendants inherited, God's perfect order had been corrupted by sin, and man himself was estranged from God. All forms of sin had this alienating effect: here is a description of one of them, in the translation (1586) of de la Primaudaye's *The French Academy*:

> God hath made man of a mild and communicable nature, apt to society, and to live with company, not solitarily, as savage beasts use to do. Therefore there is nothing more contrary to his nature, and to that end for which he was created, than this vicious pride, whereby he is so puffed up and swelleth in such sort, as if he were some other nature and condition than human, and as though he meant to live in some other estate and degree than of man.

By sinning, man lost his right-relationship with God, with the other members of his kind, with his higher self; he lost his real identity as a human being, just as he had lost his paradisal home, because he had denied his role in the pattern. Because he was a fallen being, man could be deceived, led to wrong choice by delusion; this wrong choice would then deform him further as he was taken over by an evil force not centred on God. In the individual, animal passion clouded right reason; in the state, usurpation and rebellion violated allegiance. Creation moved towards the wilderness described by Coriolanus:

> As if a man were author of himself
> And knew no other kin.

5, 3, 36-7

On the other hand, there was what philosophers called the Paradox of the Fortunate Fall, by which they meant that the fall made possible Christ's coming, through which there was offered a way of returning to grace. In personal terms, by making a Christ-like act of mercy, man could redeem himself, breaking the apparent circle of viciousness into which he so easily fell, and re-establishing contact with a loving God.

Clearly the more elaborate the pattern, the more appalling the confusion caused by its disruption, and the Elizabethan imagination was captured by a vision of chaos. This whole idea of the disjointing of the framework became particularly important in England towards the end of the sixteenth century, when Shakespeare was writing. This was partly because of the political conditions we described in Chapter 1, partly because of the impact of the ideas of the three men who laid most doubt on the traditional order—Copernicus, Montaigne and Machiavelli (who is apparently referred to as the incarnation of human villainy 395 times in the drama of this period!).

The illustration of this disjointing can be found in Donne's poem *The First Anniversary* (1611), where, describing a new philosophy that calls all in doubt, he writes:

> 'Tis all in pieces, all coherence gone;
> All just supply, and all relation:
> Prince, subject, father, son, are things forgot . . .

Yet it was not merely a new philosophy that questioned the relation between prince and subject, or between father and son.

This may have crystallised things at a certain time, but the same idea can be found in many earlier documents.

In Foxe's *Book of Martyrs* (1563) there is this:

> God has so placed us Englishmen here in one commonwealth, also in one church, as in one ship together; let us not mangle or divide the ship, which being divided perishes; but let every man serve with diligence and discretion in his order, wherein he is called. . . . No storm is so dangerous to a ship on the sea, as discord and disorder in a commonwealth; the countries, nations, kingdoms, empires, cities, towns, and houses, that have been dissolved by discord, is so manifest in history, that I need not spend time in rehearsing examples.

The passage already quoted (p. 100) from the 1547 Homily continues in these words:

> For where there is no right order, there reigneth all abuse, carnal liberty, enormity, sin and Babylonical confusion. Take away kings, princes, rulers, magistrates, judges and such states of God's order, no man shall ride or go by the highway unrobbed, no man shall sleep in his own house or bed unkilled, no man shall keep his wife, children and possessions in quietness; all things shall be common, and there must needs follow all mischief and utter destruction, both of souls, bodies, goods and commonwealths.

In the 1574 edition of the *Mirror for Magistrates* (1559) prudence, justice and temperance are seen as the virtues preventing man from becoming 'beastly and desperate':

> For to covet without consideration, to pass the measure of his degree, and to let will run at random, is the only destruction of all estates. Else how were it possible so many learned, politic, wise, renowned, valiant and victorious personages might ever have come to such utter decay?

In the academic play *Gorboduc* (1561), a speaker declares that by certain rules which 'kind' has fixed in the human spirit,

> . . . Nature hath her order and her course,
> Which being broken doth corrupt the state
> Of minds and things, even in the best of all.

Shakespeare could well have read the passages we have quoted in this section; even if he did not, they represent a pattern of ideas which it would have been as difficult for him to ignore as it would for us to ignore the work of Marx or Freud—even though we haven't read *Capital* or *Psychopathology of Everyday Life*.

SHAKESPEARE AND THE PATTERN

We suggest that a possible way of approaching Shakespeare's plays is to see them as concerned with the creation and destruction of love. It is not that each play falls entirely into one category or the other, although it is reasonable to argue that the emphasis in, say, *A Midsummer Night's Dream* or *As You Like It* is different from that in *Hamlet* or *Othello*. The conflict between the forces for and against love, as in the psychomachia of the morality plays discussed in Chapter 1, is usually fundamental to each play—*Romeo and Juliet* is perhaps the clearest example. But Shakespeare stresses one rather than the other. We want here to define these forces as he presents them, in fairly general terms, before going on to look at some plays in more detail.

The words of widest meaning that Shakespeare uses are 'nature', 'kindness' and their opposites. Because of the difficulties involved in using the word 'nature' (it's one of the most ambiguous words in the language; see the relevant chapter in C. S. Lewis's *Studies in Words*), it is helpful to note how Shakespeare uses 'kind' and 'unkind'. For him the idea of 'kindness' meant not merely being generous and fairly nice, but also suggested that quality which makes a man human, a proper man, a member of a 'kind' which is not animal. When Lady Macbeth deplores 'the milk of human kindness' in her husband, she does not merely mean that she wishes him to stop being considerate, but to stop being one of man-kind and become a monster.

In the world of kindness there rule what are listed, again in *Macbeth*, as the king-becoming virtues: justice, verity, temperance, stableness, perseverance, bounty, mercy, lowliness, devotion, patience, courage, fortitude. We might add charity, grace, honour and allegiance. All these are implied by kindness and love. Because he was a poet and not a philosopher, Shakespeare used certain symbols or images to express the same thing: a carefully tended garden, a well-tuned instrument, the ability to sleep, a banquet, the relationship of father and child, the rule of the rightful heir—above all, wooing and 'that blessed bond of board and bed' which was the marriage to which wooing led.

In Shakespeare's plays, this world of order and civility is attacked by some form of monstrosity. The idea of a malign beast attacking a human settlement has been used in English literature from Grendel in *Beowulf* to the Things from Outer Space in modern science-fiction. Milton's Satan is probably the most famous example of the type, but it is interesting to find the same figure appearing in the morality plays. In one called *Wisdom Who is Christ* (*c.* 1470) there is a Lucifer who says:

> I shall now steer his mind
> To that sin made me a fiend,
> Pride, which is against kind,
> And of sins (the) head;
> So to covetise he shall wend,
> For that endureth to the last end;
> And on to lechery, and I may him rend,
> Then am I seker [i.e. certain] the soul is dead.

It may be that a man chooses wrongly, misled by appearances, and many suffer for his mistake; it may be that some men deliberately place themselves beyond the rules of the kind, and set about the destruction of others. There is the horror of a world regressing to barbarism, turned topsy-turvy as quick, bright things come to confusion: roles are reversed, normal values become meaningless, trusts are broken, kings are killed. Humanity begins to prey on itself like the monsters of the deep; the state, the family, the individual disintegrate, and human life enters an animal-infested wilderness. The blood and baseness of our natures (ironically, because he is the basest of all villains, the explanation is Iago's) lead us to preposterous conclusions. In this world, men place 'policy' (meaning, for the Elizabethans, underhand cunning) above conscience; they dispense with pity, allowing revenge to triumph over forgiveness, letting fear and suspicion replace love. To describe this, Shakespeare uses images such as those of a storm, of the sea inundating the land, of a tree hacked down, a garden running to seed, a musical discord, a disease, a wrenching apart; there is blood, darkness, rebellion, lechery, murder, banishment.

It is as he enters this kind of hell that Othello tells Desdemona that their love, 'the fountain from the which my current runs, Or else dries up', is being transformed into 'a cistern for foul toads To knot and gender in'; it is in a similar plight that Hamlet accuses his mother of an act which 'takes off the rose From the fair forehead of an innocent love, And sets a blister there'; Timon declares: '. . . All's oblique; There's nothing level in our cursed natures But direct villainy'.

Shakespeare wrote, in *A Midsummer Night's Dream*: 'Things base and vile, holding no quantity, Love can transpose to form and dignity'; on another occasion, in *Richard the Second* he wrote that 'foul sin gathering head Shall break into corruption'. These are the fundamental poles within which Shakespeare's plays as a whole operate. One modern critic, John Vyvyan, (see the Reading List on p. 140) has said that all Shakespeare's leading characters are wayfarers on a road; at the bottom is the tragic act leading to chaos and death; at the top is a loving act of creative mercy leading to a rebirth of order. Each protagonist is made to face a choice, a temptation, to which his response is critical. If he accepts the guidance of fidelity and love, the world of kindness is maintained; if these are rejected, the soul is taken over by retrograde passions, and an originally noble nature finds itself committed to an ignoble deed. These plays depend on the fundamental assumptions that a man must learn to distinguish good and evil; that it is only the good, in the form of love, justice, mercy and loyalty, that makes possible civilised life. They ask the question: 'What is a man to do?'

THE VISION OF HORROR

W. B. Yeats once said that the central thing about Shakespeare was his vision of horror. Shakespeare's most famous general description of horror is in the so-called 'order speech' in *Troilus and Cressida*. Ulysses is telling the Greek chiefs of staff that the war against Troy is going badly because they have neglected the 'specialty of rule', by which is meant the whole function of ordered government. Ulysses shows how all the aspects of order —'degree, priority, and place, Insisture, course, proportion, season, form, Office and custom'—are observed in the solar system; how, when planets 'in evil mixture to disorder wander', there is a horrible commotion which will 'rend and deracinate, The unity and married calm of states Quite from their fixture'. Then, using so many of the images we have mentioned, relating the cosmological, political and personal aspects of the Elizabethan world picture, he goes on:

> How could communities,
> Degrees in schools, and brotherhoods in cities,
> Peaceful commerce from dividable shores,
> The primogenity and due of birth,
> Prerogative of age, crowns, sceptres, laurels,
> But by degree, stand in authentic place?
> Take but degree away, untune that string,
> And hark what discord follows! Each thing melts
> In mere oppugnancy: the bounded waters
> Should lift their bosoms higher than the shores,
> And make a sop of all this solid globe;
> Strength should be lord of imbecility,
> And the rude son should strike his father dead;
> Force should be right; or, rather, right and wrong—
> Between whose endless jar justice resides—
> Should lose their names, and so should justice too.
> Then everything includes itself in power,
> Power into will, will into appetite;
> And appetite, an universal wolf,
> So doubly seconded with will and power,
> Must make perforce an universal prey,
> And last eat up himself.

I, 3, 103-24

Similarly the Duke in *Measure for Measure* notes that in Vienna the 'strict statutes and most biting laws, The needful bits and curbs to headstrong steeds' have ceased to operate:

> ... so our decrees,
> Dead to infliction, to themselves are dead;
> And liberty plucks justice by the nose;
> The baby beats the nurse, and quite athwart
> Goes all decorum.

I, 3, 27-31

When, in *Timon of Athens*, Timon leaves the city—an 'ingrateful seat of monstrous friends'—for the woods where he expects to 'find Th' unkindest beast more kinder than mankind', he prays that the human settlement shall be given over to the dominion of Ulysses' 'universal wolf':

> Piety and fear,
> Religion to the gods, peace, justice, truth,
> Domestic awe, night-rest, and neighbourhood,
> Instruction, manners, mysteries, and trades,
> Degrees, observances, customs and laws,
> Decline to your confounding contraries
> And let confusion live.

4, 1, 15-21

When this vision of horror occupies his mind, Shakespeare's plays are full of plotting, crime, war, violent death. All the drama we are going to discuss in this section could be summarised in the way Horatio describes the events of *Hamlet*:

> So shall you hear
> Of carnal, bloody, and unnatural acts;
> Of accidental judgments, casual slaughters;
> Of deaths put on by cunning and forc'd cause ...

5, 2, 372-5

Or in the terms of Antony's prophecy over the dead body of the ruler of Rome in *Julius Caesar*:

> Domestic fury and fierce civil strife
> Shall cumber all the parts of Italy;
> Blood and destruction shall be so in use,

And dreadful objects so familiar,
That mothers shall but smile when they behold
Their infants quartered with the hands of war,
All pity chok'd with custom of fell deeds. . . .

3, 1, 264-70

What is truly remarkable is the consistency and continuity in these descriptions of horror. Shakespeare repeats characters and situations in the way that certain painters may be obsessed for years by a face, a particular view or group of objects. For example, the canon more or less begins and ends with plays containing a 'vile man': Jack Cade in *2 Henry the Sixth*, Caliban in *The Tempest*, both leading rebellions against the ruler, both intent on destroying the formal law and learning represented by books, both attempting to invert the hierarchy by setting the labourer up as a magistrate. Throughout the plays there are people who will not accept the rules of the kind: Aaron in *Titus Andronicus*, Richard III, Lady Macbeth, Iago, Edmund, Sebastian and Antonio in *The Tempest*. Again and again there are men lost in the conflict of irreconcilable worlds: Hamlet, Othello, Lear, Coriolanus, Antony in *Antony and Cleopatra*. Repeatedly we see one character urging another to violence: the king and Buckingham in *Richard the Third*, John and Hubert in *King John*, Cassius and Brutus, Don John and Claudio in *Much Ado About Nothing*, Lady Macbeth and her husband, Iago and Othello, Leontes and Camillo in *The Winter's Tale*, Posthumus and Pisanio in *Cymbeline*. Repeatedly we are shown people—usually the heroines—victimised by slander: Hero in *Much Ado About Nothing*, Desdemona, Edgar, Imogen in *Cymbeline*, Hermione in *The Winter's Tale*.

As early as 1594 Shakespeare had given a characteristic statement of this destruction of love when he described how Tarquin went to rape Lucrece:

Here with a cockatrice' dead-killing eye
He rouseth up himself, and makes a pause;
While she, the picture of pure piety,
Like a white hind under the grype's sharp claws,
Pleads, in a wilderness where are no laws,

To the rough beast that knows no gentle right,
Nor aught obeys but his foul appetite.

THE RAPE OF LUCRECE, 540-6

The plays are for much of their length concerned with the chaos of such a wilderness where there is no law. They show this wilderness operating on a public or political level, and a private or psychological one—one of Shakespeare's main points being that the one leads to the other. But there is love as well as horror in most of them; in fact, we might say that the horror makes sense only in so far as it is a destruction of love. Ulysses' warning about the depredations of a universal wolf is meaningful only if you realise the nature of the 'specialty of rule'. The sense of disorder in that speech must be put alongside the sense of order in this one (from a part of *Henry the Eighth* usually ascribed to Shakespeare) where the pageantry at the Field of the Cloth of Gold is being described:

> All was royal:
> To the disposing of it nought rebell'd;
> Order gave each thing view. The office did
> Distinctly his full function.

I, 1, 42-5

In the discussions of the plays which follow, as far as possible Shakespeare's own words and images are used, without quotation marks. The diligent reader will recognise most of them.

THE HISTORIES

Shakespeare deals with the upsetting of order on the public or political level in the Histories, where the real hero is England, rather than the various kings after whom individual plays are named. They are an elaboration of a sentence Shakespeare saw in one of his main sources (Hall's *History*): 'As by discord great things decay and fall, so the same by concord be revived and erected'. In *Hamlet* Claudius is told of a 'cease of majesty' which 'Dies not alone, but like a gulf doth draw What's near it with it'; the histories deal with the actual or possible cessation of sovereignty as a principle of order in the commonwealth, and with the consequent gulf of horror.

The First Tetralogy

The first group of histories (the three parts of *Henry the Sixth* and *Richard the Third*) shows the destruction of England's honour, under a king whose holy virtue makes him politically ineffectual when surrounded by wilfully disobedient, proud and malicious nobles, each seeking personal preferment rather than the preservation of the realm. There is the loss of France, the death of the heroic and loyal Talbot, the quarrels over the succession ('unkind division'), the sequence of killing and counter-killing leading to those Wars of the Roses which reduced a kingdom to a slaughter-house. The ideals of service, oath-keeping, and allegiance are replaced by civil dissension— 'a viperous worm That gnaws the bowels of the commonwealth'. A nobleman tells the king in *2 Henry the Sixth*:

> Ah, gracious lord, these days are dangerous!
> Virtue is chok'd with foul ambition,
> And charity chas'd hence by rancour's hand;
> Foul subornation is predominant,
> And equity exil'd your Highness' land.

3, 1, 142-6

From this background emerge figures like the usurper York; like Cade (a stock Elizabethan symbol of the rebel), with his Kentish followers 'in order when we are most out of order'; like the son-killing father and the father-killing son who meet on the battle-field at Towton. Above all there emerges the figure of Richard III: king-killer, crooked in shape and nature, said to be born with teeth—a monstrousness which he accepts and boasts of as something putting him beyond the 'kind'. This is the first of Shakespeare's large-scale studies of those who deny love:

> And so I was, which plainly signified
> That I should snarl, and bite, and play the dog.
> Then, since the heavens have shap'd my body so,
> Let hell make crook'd my mind to answer it.

I have no brother, I am like no brother;
And this word 'love', which greybeards call divine,
Be resident in men like one another,
And not in me! I am myself alone.

3 HENRY THE SIXTH, 5, 6, 76-83

To Richard, conscience—man's higher nature—is merely a
word which tries to make him a coward; the sword is his law.
To his destroyer this makes him simply a beast:

The wretched, bloody, and usurping boar,
That spoil'd your summer fields and fruitful vines,
Swills your warm blood like wash, and makes his trough
In your embowell'd bosoms. . . .

RICHARD THE THIRD, 5, 2, 7-10

Once the monster is dead (and the situation will be repeated in
Macbeth), smooth-faced peace returns and the civil wounds are
healed; the madness, butchery, self-scarring and dire division
are over.

The Second Tetralogy

In the second group (*Richard the Second*, the two parts of
Henry the Fourth, and *Henry the Fifth*), England's story is
taken up at an earlier stage, moving from a disastrous to an
ideal king.

Richard's unstaid youth will not listen to wholesome counsel
because his ears are stopped by flattering vanity; he acts wilfully
in a rash fierce blaze of riot; in depriving the exiled Bolingbroke
of his patrimony he denies the principle of succession by which
he himself has become king. Thus the ideal England of Gaunt's
'sceptred-isle' speech is destroyed. The royal gardeners make
crystal clear the message of the play as they go about their
tasks of tending and pruning:

Why should we, in the compass of a pale,
Keep law and form and due proportion,
Showing, as in a model, our firm estate,
When our sea-walled garden, the whole land,
Is full of weeds; her fairest flowers chok'd up,
Her fruit trees all unprun'd, her hedges ruin'd,

Her knots disordered, and her wholesome herbs
Swarming with caterpillars?

RICHARD THE SECOND, 3, *4*, 40-7

In the following rebellion, when Richard's night becomes
Bolingbroke's fair day, there is the familiar disintegration of
authority and inversion of hierarchical order: the night-owl
shrieks where the mounting lark should sing; a ruler, born to
command but now plume-plucked, descends into a base-court
where he must sue; the lion has to kiss the rod like a schoolboy.
Richard is stage-managed by Bolingbroke in an inverted coronation ceremony; this is the scene—omitted from all the versions
printed in Elizabeth's time—that played its strange part in the
Essex rebellion (see p. 23). He is made to deny his sacred state;
glory is made base, sovereignty a slave. But the new king is
warned that in replacing the figure of God's majesty he is destroying ordered sequence as surely as ever Richard himself did
when he prevented Bolingbroke from succeeding to his father's
estates. The result will be a wilderness:

> The blood of English shall manure the ground,
> And future ages groan for this foul act;
> Peace shall go sleep with Turks and infidels,
> And in this seat of peace tumultuous wars
> Shall kin with kin and kind with kind confound;
> Disorder, horror, fear, and mutiny,
> Shall here inhabit. . . .

RICHARD THE SECOND, 4, *1*, 137-43

Henry the Fifth gives a complementary picture of the mirror of
all Christian kings, full of grace and fair regard, ripe for great
exploits, governing a commonwealth like that of the bees, who
by a rule in nature teach the act of order to a peopled kingdom.
At home he destroys incipient rebellion with a terrible and
constant resolution; abroad he acts the royal captain, putting
men's hearts into the trim on the eve of Agincourt. At the end
of *Richard the Second* the new king, Henry IV, had regarded the
unthrifty son who was to succeed him as a wanton and effeminate
boy, taking it as honourable to support a dissolute crew. At the

beginning of *Henry the Fifth* it is made clear that this wildness is dead: the man addicted to vain courses has had the offending Adam whipped out of him, leaving his body as a paradise to be inhabited by celestial spirits.

This fundamental reformation and achieving of the specialty of rule is studied in *Henry the Fourth*, the two parts of which are largely about the education of a future king in the principles of honour and justice, about his rejection of a temptation to misrule which, if accepted, would have brought England into chaos.

The background to this education is again rebellion. One of the rebels, also a leader of the earlier rebellion against Richard (one of Shakespeare's points is that violence breeds violence), makes a familiar statement:

> Let heaven kiss earth! Now let not Nature's hand
> Keep the wild flood confin'd! Let order die!
> And let this world no longer be a stage
> To feed contention in a ling'ring act;
> But let one spirit of the first-born Cain
> Reign in all bosoms, that, each heart being set
> On bloody courses, the rude scene may end
> And darkness be the burier of the dead!
>
> 2 HENRY THE FOURTH, I, *1*, 153-60

Hal has to choose true honour, as opposed to the egotistic recklessness of Hotspur or the cynicism of Falstaff; he has to choose the way of law, represented by the Lord Chief Justice, rather than the way of misrule, represented again by a Falstaff who follows the young prince like an evil angel, a reverend vice, grey iniquity, abominable misleader of youth, old white-bearded Satan. Falstaff's life of disease, lechery, drunkenness, swindling and theft is as much a preying on the commonwealth as the Machiavellian tactics of the lords in *Henry the Sixth*.

Shakespeare makes the direction of the play clear from the start when Hal explains that he upholds the unyoked humour of idle companions only to appear the more glorious when he casts them off—as the sun may be more wondered at 'By breaking through the foul and ugly mists Of vapours that did seem to

strangle him'. But to his father, the successor's brow seems
stained by riot and dishonour; his princely privilege lost by
participation in the vile. The dying Henry IV envisages what
England will be with this apparent failure of rule:

> Pluck down my officers, break my decrees;
> For now a time is come to mock at form—
> Harry the Fifth is crown'd. Up, vanity:
> Down, royal state. All you sage counsellors, hence.
> And to the English court assemble now,
> From every region, apes of idleness.
> ....
> For the fifth Harry from curb'd license plucks
> The muzzle of restraint, and the wild dog
> Shall flesh his tooth on every innocent.
> O my poor kingdom, sick with civil blows!
> When that my care could not withhold thy riots,
> What wilt thou do when riot is thy care?
> O, thou wilt be a wilderness again,
> Peopled with wolves, thy old inhabitants!
>
> 2 HENRY THE FOURTH, 4, *5*, 118-38

But the cease of majesty is only apparent. At the battle of
Shrewsbury Hal had temporarily redeemed his reputation, no
longer being a truant to chivalry; then he had cured the wounds
of his intemperance, showing himself so little in love with vanity
that even the rebels admitted England had never owned so
sweet a hope, so much misconstrued in his wantonness. Similarly,
in the second part of the play, the fears of the Lord Chief Justice
after the death of Henry IV are shown to be groundless: the
new ruler accepts Justice as a father; the tide of blood, recently
flowing in vanity, now turns to run in majesty. Falstaff is rejected
in the words 'I know thee not, old man'; the tutor and feeder of
riot, the misleader of the king's former self, is banished.

THE TRAGEDIES

In the tragedies written between 1600 and 1608 which are the
climax of his work, Shakespeare follows the same vision. Here
the misleaders are not banished; the wilderness of wolves and

the chaos of misrule become at least temporary realities. Public and political considerations are not ignored (*Macbeth* is as much a picture of a disrupted commonwealth as *Henry the Sixth*) but the interest seems to be mainly on the personal causes and effects of horror. Here we see the operation of what Hamlet calls a man's 'vicious mole of nature'—the individual's capacity for evil, when passion perverts judgment; and his capacity to be betrayed by evil, particularly in the form of what is referred to in *The Merchant of Venice* as 'the seeming truth which cunning times put on To entrap the wisest'. These plays—*Julius Caesar, Hamlet, Othello, Macbeth* and *Antony and Cleopatra; King Lear* is left for later consideration—illustrate a couplet from *Measure for Measure*:

> O, what may man within him hide,
> Though angel on the outward side!

3, 2, 253-4

Or this passage from *Romeo and Juliet* where Friar Lawrence discusses the poisonous and medicinal properties of herbs:

> Two such opposed kings encamp them still
> In man as well as herbs—grace and rude will;
> And where the worser is predominant,
> Full soon the canker death eats up that plant.

2, 3, 27-30

Their heroes can be seen as one of the characters in *Henry the Eighth* sees Buckingham: a man 'so complete Who was enroll'd 'mongst wonders' but who, it appears:

> Hath into monstrous habits put the graces
> That once were his, and is become as black
> As if besmear'd in hell.

I, 2, 122-4

Julius Caesar

Thus, Brutus' honourable metal is moulded by the envious Cassius from its true disposition—'For who so firm that cannot be seduc'd?' As a result, Brutus, while admitting that he has not known when Caesar's passions have got the better of his reason, and that he knows no personal cause to spurn at him, agrees to an assassination for the sake of a vague future political security. Coming to such a decision for him is to feel chaos in his own mind; between the first thought of an evil act and its performance there is a hideous dream when the state of man suffers the nature of an insurrection. Brutus joins a conspiracy whose monstrous visage must, like that of Claudius, Iago, Macbeth or Edmund, hide itself in smiles and affability. The noblest Roman of them all, whose elements were so mixed that Nature might stand up and say to all the world 'This was a man!', is involved in an evil which destroys him, and creates the civil disorder described by Antony in the passage quoted on page 112.

Hamlet

'A little more than kin, and less than kind'—Hamlet's first words, in reply to his uncle-stepfather's reference to him as both cousin and son, show immediately the bewilderment of a man whose family relationship has been destroyed. His mother has posted with dexterity to incestuous sheets ('O such a deed As from the body of contraction plucks The very soul'); his uncle—if a ghost can be believed—has murdered the king who was Hamlet's father. From the sin of Claudius ('this canker of our nature') there spreads a disease, a rottenness in the Danish state which involves everybody. The world has become a place where one may smile, and smile, and yet be a bloody, bawdy, treacherous, lecherous, kindless villain; the place is a prison, and the time is out of joint. The royal court, where more than anywhere else there should be specialty of rule, becomes a place where no one can trust any one else, where there is incessant spying and play-acting, intriguing and counter-intriguing.

In this world, Hamlet, who has promised to let the ghost's commandment to revenge live alone in his brain, finds himself benetted round with villainies, his own imaginings as foul as Vulcan's stithy. Ophelia describes his coming to her 'As if he had been loosed out of Hell To speak of horrors'; she later sees him as the noblest of men, 'Th' expectancy and rose of the fair state, The glass of fashion and the mould of form', who has been destroyed. His sovereign reason is jangled like bells out of tune; the 'unmatch'd form and feature of blown youth' is blasted. Hamlet himself, when most of his kind, except for Horatio, seem to be acting like monsters, is obsessed by ideas of disease and death, paralysed one moment by a world that has lost all meaning, driven the next to hysterical action. All the uses of the world have become weary, stale, flat and unprofitable; the earth is like an unweeded garden in which everything has gone to seed, and which is utterly possessed by things rank and gross in nature. Noble man, the climax of creation, seems vile; the fair, to use the imagery of *Macbeth*, has become foul:

> I have of late—but wherefore I know not—lost all my mirth, foregone all custom of exercises; and indeed it goes so heavily with my disposition that this goodly frame, the earth, seems to me a sterile promontory; this most excellent canopy the air, look you, this brave o'er-hanging firmament, this majestical roof fretted with golden fire—why, it appeareth no other thing to me than a foul and pestilent congregation of vapours. What a piece of work is a man! How noble in reason! how infinite in faculties! in form and moving, how express and admirable! in action, how like an angel! in apprehension, how like a god! the beauty of the world! the paragon of animals! And yet, to me, what is this quintessence of dust? Man delights not me. . . .
>
> 2, 2, 295-307

In this disrupted condition it seems to Hamlet that he must be cruel to be kind—an inversion of what seems to be Shakespeare's central belief that only love and forgiveness can create 'kindness'. He becomes a man hovering on the brink of animality: 'Now could I drink hot blood, And do such bitter business as the day Would quake to look on'. It is in vain that he attempts to modify this statement by adding: 'O heart, lose not thy nature. . . . Let me be cruel, not unnatural'. The cruelty leads to the rejection, insanity and death of the girl who loves him; to the scene with his mother; to the killing of Polonius; to the killing of a king in revenge for that same crime; to death at the hands of another son, Laertes, revenging his own murdered father. It is a chaos almost as symmetrically patterned as the Elizabethan World Picture itself. The man who was likely to have proved most royal, has died in a shambles—for which he has been partly responsible—more becoming a battlefield than a court.

Othello

Othello at the beginning is majestic, of great reputation, far more fair than black, his life and being derived from men of royal position. He marries a woman bearing all the excellence of creation, for whom storms and rocks renounce their destructive natures. Reunited to this 'divine Desdemona' in Cyprus, Othello declares that death would now be happiness because his soul has a content so absolute 'That not another comfort like to this Succeeds in unknown fate'. The wife prays that their love and comfort may increase daily; the husband hopes that their kissing will be the greatest discord between them.

This well-tuned music is destroyed by Iago to whom 'kindness' in its main forms of love and service is meaningless. For him, one who serves another becomes a beast of burden; he himself merely puts on a mask of duty while seeking self-advancement. Love is merely animal mating; trust is something that can be exploited; to be of a free and open nature like Othello is merely to be tenderly led by the nose like an ass. Iago is the devil, putting on the blackest sin, but suggesting goodness at first with heavenly shows.

These shows poison Othello's love. Because he cannot distinguish truth from falsehood, his joy in Desdemona is made to lose its colour, and he enters the world of horror, bestiality, and blood. He loses self-control as passion overcomes him; he is deprived of that sweet sleep which Shakespeare used so often to suggest right-relationship. If Desdemona is false, as Othello believes her to be, then heaven seems to mock itself. All meaning vanishes, along with the tranquil mind, the big wars that make ambition virtue; Othello has lost his occupation, and once his clear spirit is puddled he becomes a devil. His bosom is said to be full of aspics' tongues; his mind is compared to a plaguehouse. He expels love:

> All my fond love thus do I blow to heaven.
> 'Tis gone.
> Arise, black vengeance, from the hollow hell.
> Yield up, O love, thy crown and hearted throne
> To tyrannous hate!

3, 3, 449-53

Thus degraded (and the two scenes (3, 3 and 4, 1) in which this occurs are perhaps the most horrifying in Shakespeare) Othello becomes an animal, wishing to tear Desdemona to pieces. In his degradation he tries to bring Desdemona to the same level: instead of being wheeled about with graces, her virtue is apparently turned to pitch, and her very goodness becomes the net to enmesh them all.

Villainy, as Emilia says, has made mocks with love. Othello is made to realise that, ignorant as dirt, he has fallen to the cunning of a damned slave. Being worked upon, perplexed in the extreme, he has thrown away his jewel like an ignorant savage. He sees himself as one whipped by devils from the possession of a heavenly sight, blown in winds, roasted in sulphur, washed in gulfs of liquid fire. 'When I love thee not, Chaos is come again': Othello's words are one of the central statements of Shakespearean tragedy.

Macbeth

Macbeth begins as valour's minion, fighting honourably as a defender of the king against rebel and invader, declaring that it is his only duty to do everything for the safety of Duncan's love and honour. The apparently faithful servant is rewarded, planted, and promised future growth. But already Macbeth has seen the weird sisters; his mind toys with a suggestion 'Whose horrid image doth unfix my hair And make my seated heart knock at my ribs Against the use of nature'. He is on the road leading to the denial of kindness: 'For mine own good all causes shall give way'.

Allying himself with evil in the person of Lady Macbeth, who cuts herself off from humankind by asking to be unsexed by the murdering ministers that wait on nature's mischief, Macbeth kills a king staying with him in a double trust. By doing more than may become a man, he destroys renown and grace, makes a breach in the natural order for ruin's wasteful entrance, creates confusion's masterpiece. He defiles his own mind with evil, just as irrevocably as his wife stains her hands with blood. His mind is filled with scorpions; he seems a dwarfish thief dressed in a giant's clothes; he finds that things badly begun can make themselves strong only by further badness. He has waded beyond the point of no return into a river of blood.

Once Macbeth has alienated himself from love, service, loyalty and the other king-becoming virtues, he is willing to see the whole frame of things disjoint; the honour, love, obedience and troops of friends which would have been his in an ordered world are replaced by curses and a mere show of respect. Since he cannot buckle a distempered cause within the belt of rule, life is meaningless—a tale told by an idiot.

By his unnatural deed, Macbeth creates a world where the fair and foul cannot be distinguished, where you may look like a flower but act like the serpent under it, where a false face hides what the false heart knows. Here all values are inverted. Macbeth asks for a blessing while he is killing; after Duncan's death horses contend against obedience, and a falcon at the highest point of its flight is killed by an owl. Lady Macduff, for whom life is a wild and violent sea in which she floats without direction, reminds herself before she is killed that in this world it is often laudable to do harm, and considered dangerously foolish to do good (it is instructive to compare her speech—4, 2—with the words of the Homily quoted on p. 107).

Scotland, suffering under a hand accursed, is a place of blood, darkness and reverberating emptiness. There are bloody knives at banquets, and nights are sleepless; there is neither faithful homage nor free honour. New sorrows strike heaven in the face, and good men's lives expire before the flowers in their hats. A tyrant, topping in damnation all the devils of horrid hell, has created a country that is a grave rather than a mother. Death has driven out love, and majesty has ceased.

Antony and Cleopatra

Here there is folly rather than horror, and majesty ceases in one form only to be found in another. At the beginning, Antony, once the triple pillar of the world, is seen as a man transformed into a strumpet's fool, renouncing all restraint to become the fan and bellows to cool a gipsy's lust. In choosing Egypt rather than Rome he has made an ignoble swerving which has offended reputation; his captainship is nicked by passion, when will dominates reason. At the shameful defeat of Actium, to which his following of Cleopatra has led, 'Experience, manhood, honour, ne'er before Did violate so itself'.

Antony himself tells Octavius that poisoned hours have kept him from a knowledge of his own self; he feels imprisoned in strong Egyptian fetters. After his military defeat he knows that his fortunes are corrupting honest men like Enobarbus; he has been beguiled to the very heart of loss by one he trusted—the Cleopatra 'Whose bosom was my crownet, my chief end'. Apparently caught in a chaos of irreconcilable demands, Antony could be speaking for Brutus, Hamlet, Othello or Macbeth when he says:

> But when we in our viciousness grow hard—
> O misery on't!—the wise gods seel our eyes,
> In our own filth drop our clear judgments, make us
> Adore our errors, laugh at's while we strut
> To our confusion.

3, 13, 111-5

But to leave the play there would be completely misleading. The Roman world of order which Antony has betrayed is seen as something rather cold, characterised by war and a petty political chaffering which uses marriage as an affair of business. Egypt may mean Antony's noble ruin, but it means magic as well. Antony himself describes 'kingdoms' (political power) as clay—the real nobleness of life is to love. To Cleopatra, the man who died after a bungled suicide-attempt, itself the result of her childish lying, is a supreme hero, with no winter in his bounty. Similarly, Cleopatra herself is a lass unparalleled as well as a right gipsy, one who makes hungry again the appetite she has satisfied. 'For vilest things become themselves [i.e. make themselves comely or beautiful] in her.' Confronted with the dying Antony, her desolation—'Shall I abide In this dull world, which in thy absence is No better than a sty?'—begins to make a better life. Cleopatra dies dressed as a queen 'marble constant' and transfigured by love:

> Husband, I come.
> Now to that name my courage prove my title!
> I am fire and air; my other elements
> I give to baser life.

5, 2, 285-8

This is one of the most beautiful scenes in Shakespeare. It is as if his celebration of the triumph of love over worldly chaos—an empty triumph in material terms—moved him to produce some of his greatest dramatic poetry.

In *Venus and Adonis* Shakespeare made a distinction between lust and love in the following way:

> Love comforteth like sunshine after rain,
> But Lust's effect is tempest after sun;
> Love's gentle spring doth always fresh remain:
> Lust's winter comes ere summer half be done.
> Love surfeits not: Lust like a glutton dies.
> Love is all truth: Lust full of forged lies.

799-804

In a play of about the same time, like *Antony and Cleopatra* concerned with love in a world of violence, Shakespeare made Juliet describe her bounty as boundless as the sea, her love as deep: 'the more I give to thee The more I have, for both are infinite'. It is this unlimited bounty of love which is represented by Cleopatra, and it is this which we must now discuss.

THE VISION OF LOVE

It is important to remember that although chaos is glimpsed

in all those plays which are largely concerned with horror, Shakespeare in the end reasserts the rule of law and the existence of order. Troilus in his anguish at the deception of Cressida declares that 'the bonds of heaven are slipp'd, dissolv'd and loos'd'; and in the plays we have just been describing we see this happening again and again. But by the end, some form of bond has been re-established. The two groups of histories lead up to Richmond and Henry V; the tragedies end with order reimposed by the Roman triumvirate, or Fortinbras, or Cassio, or Malcolm.

The comedies and the romances are the plays that show most clearly how, through love and forgiveness, bonds are formed; or it may be better to say re-formed, because even in these plays there are suggestions of the tragic world, if only because the course of true love never did run smooth. For example, in *The Two Gentlemen of Verona* Proteus betrays his friend and the woman he is supposed to love; Valentine suffers exile, joining a band of outlaws who 'make their wills their laws'. In *A Midsummer Night's Dream* there is the dispute between Titania and Oberon with its 'progeny of evils'. In *As You Like It* there is a usurping duke exiling his brother, niece and daughter, and another man is driven into the forest by 'the malice Of a diverted blood and bloody brother'. Even in *Twelfth Night* there is this description of a familiar tragic fact:

> In nature there's no blemish but the mind:
> None can be call'd deform'd but the unkind.
> Virtue is beauty; but the beauteous evil
> Are empty trunks, o'erflourish'd by the devil.

3, 4, 351-4

But if these elements are present, they are what the plays of this type are moving away from. The direction of the comedies and the romances is towards that kind of bond which is described in the last line of *The Two Gentlemen of Verona*: 'One feast, one house, one mutual happiness'. Here the action is largely concerned with wooing and marriage. In *Love's Labour's Lost* five marriages are to be celebrated; in *A Midsummer Night's Dream* and

128

Twelfth Night three; in *As You Like It* there are four, together with an exile ended, a daughter restored to her father, and two sets of brothers reconciled. These plays show men moving to a true idea of love, away from one that is false; Benedick in *Much Ado About Nothing* is a good example. Here the heroines, who in the tragedies were destroyed, are supreme—because they represent love.

There are in these plays many statements on the power of such love. In *The Two Gentlemen of Verona* it is seen as a divine instructor—'There is no woe in his correction, Nor to his service no such joy on earth'—and to be exiled from the vision of love is to have the self destroyed. In this same play, Valentine says the following of Silvia (it is what Othello meant when he said that chaos came when he loved not Desdemona):

> ... banish'd from her
> Is self from self, a deadly banishment.
> What light is light, if Silvia be not seen?
> What joy is joy if Silvia be not by?
> Unless it be to think that she is by,
> And feed upon the shadow of perfection.

> 3, 1, 172-7

In *Love's Labour's Lost* Berowne argues that the 'leaden contemplation' of books is arid compared with the study of women's eyes, and of the love they symbolise:

> But love, first learned in a lady's eyes,
> Lives not alone immured in the brain,
> But with the motion of all elements
> Courses as swift as thought in every power,
> And gives to every power a double power,
> Above their functions and their offices.

> 4, 3, 323-8

The bond of love for Shakespeare is allied to the harmony of music, which brings peace to him who hears it. In *The Merchant of Venice* Lorenzo tells Jessica how the 'savage eyes' of beasts can be 'turned to a modest gaze By the sweet power of music'.

He continues:

> The man that hath no music in himself,
> Nor is not mov'd with concord of sweet sounds,
> Is fit for treasons, stratagems, and spoils;
> The motions of his spirit are dull as night,
> And his affections dark as Erebus.
> Let no such man be trusted.

5, 1, 83-8

It is to this music in a man—his kindness—that Portia appeals in the most famous speech of the same play, when she describes the quality of mercy to one who seems to have power of life or death over another. Mere justice, she argues, would deprive all of us of salvation, and it must be seasoned by the deeds of mercy. Such mercy

> . . . is enthroned in the hearts of kings,
> It is an attribute to God himself . . .

4, 1, 189-90

The Duke in *Measure for Measure* makes a similar argument when he says that a man's virtue is important only in so far as he uses it to help others:

> Thyself and thy belongings
> Are not thine own so proper as to waste
> Thyself upon thy virtues, they on thee.
> Heaven doth with us as we with torches do,
> Not light them for themselves; for if our virtues
> Did not go forth of us, 'twere all alike
> As if we had them not.

1, 1, 30-6

These ideas of the music in man, love, forth-going virtue, and the tempering of justice by mercy, are explored most fully in Shakespeare's last plays. Their concern with the opposites of revenge, crime and death is suggested by these lines from *Cymbeline*:

> Kneel not to me.
> The pow'r that I have on you is to spare you;

The malice towards you to forgive you. Live,
And deal with others better.

5, 5, 417-20

We will take two of these last romances as detailed examples of
this vision of love.

The Winter's Tale

For most of its first half, the play seems to be moving steadily
into the world of horror—particularly into that aspect of it
already described in *Othello*. At the beginning it seems that
Leontes is only too anxious to be 'over-kind' to Polixenes:
in their past boyhood, their friendship has been an idyllic
changing of innocence for innocence, when they knew not the
doctrine of ill-doing; in the present there seems to be a 'branch-
ing affection' so deeply rooted between them that there is neither
matter nor malice in the world to alter it. But this right-relationship is disrupted because Leontes' heart, dancing with a tyrannous
passion, and his brain, infected with a diseased and dangerous
opinion, make him suspect that he has been betrayed by his
friend and his wife:

> Dost think I am so muddy, so unsettled,
> To appoint myself in this vexation; sully
> The purity and whiteness of my sheets—
> Which to preserve is sleep, which being spotted
> Is goads, thorns, nettles, tails of wasps;
> Give scandal to the blood o' th' Prince, my son—
> Who I do think is mine, and love as mine—
> Without ripe moving to't? Would I do this?
> Could man so blench?

1, 2, 325-33

In this 'blenching' (swerving from the way of reason),
Leontes, like the earlier tragic heroes, loses himself by weaving
the web of his own folly. Full of a bloody purpose which leads
to a foul issue, he destroys a friendship, banishes both his
daughter and his best counsellor, is indirectly responsible for the
death of his son and the apparent death of his wife. But Leontes

131

himself does not die at this point—as he would do if this were a tragedy. At the end of this part of the play he is made aware of his monstrous trespass; he accepts the need for perpetual shame. By showing a saint-like sorrow which redeems all faults, a penitence greater than his sin, he is able to re-create himself for the restitutions of the last act.

The second half of the play moves steadily towards these— most obviously in the long pastoral scene (4, 4). Here, despite the intrusion of another foul passion in Polixenes' threats to his son and the others, all the emphasis is on the celebration of fertility, spring, youth and love in song, feasting and dancing. There is Florizel, true to his oath of love, remaining 'heir to his affections' despite threats. There is Perdita, fairest of all women, though lacking instruction, a mistress to most that teach, the most peerless piece of earth that ever the sun shone upon. When this gracious couple stand before Leontes, this is how he addresses Florizel:

> The blessed gods
> Purge all infection from our air whilst you
> Do climate here! You have a holy father,
> A graceful gentleman, against whose person,
> So sacred as it is, I have done sin,
> For which the heavens, taking angry note,
> Have left me issueless; and your father's blest,
> As he from heaven merits it, with you,
> Worthy his goodness.

5, 1, 168-76

What we see in the following scenes is 'royalty's repair': a lost daughter is restored to her father, a friend to a friend, a counsellor to his original master, a wife—imitating a statue coming to life—to her husband. That which was dissevered has, in time and through the action of love and penitence, become whole. Love has re-created order from the chaos of evil.

The Tempest

Here the direction of the action is very similar. Before it starts, Prospero and Miranda have been exiled from their dukedom by a brother entertaining ambition, acting like the ivy sucking verdure from a princely trunk. And throughout the play the theme of usurpation is emphasised. The same brother persuades Sebastian to attempt the killing of *his* brother, King of Naples; Caliban persuades Stephano and Trinculo to undertake the savage murder of Prospero, along with the burning of his books and the rape of his daughter. Some of these men, all caring no more for the name of a king than the roarers of the storm that opens the play, are spiritually poisoned; others are physically drunk; the inverted world they wish to create is suggested by a monster's acceptance of a drunken butler as a god, and his belief that foot-licking servility is freedom.

Caliban is Shakespeare's last monster: he is a demi-devil, a thing of darkness, as disproportioned in his manners as in his shape (like Richard III, in a description written twenty years earlier). This is a nature in whom nurture, education in civility and love, cannot stick; pains humanely taken on him are lost; his vile race has that in it which good natures cannot abide to be with. Stripes or lashing may move him but not 'kindness'. Yet even this monster is less monstrous than the human beings who have renounced their humanity; for him the island is full of sweet noises inaudible to the other usurpers; unlike them, he realises what a thrice-double ass he has been, and ends by saying that he will be wise hereafter, seeking for grace.

This grace is represented by the non-vile, or noble, characters: Gonzalo, who acted as a loyal sir to the master he once followed, Prospero, Miranda and Ferdinand. It is the relationship of these last three, to one another and to Ariel, that forms the play's vision of love.

Prospero himself learns from the spirit Ariel (it is very different from what Hamlet or Macbeth heard) to make his passions tender, to be 'kindly moved' against those who have wronged him:

> Though with their high wrongs I am struck to th' quick,
> Yet with my nobler reason 'gainst my fury
> Do I take part; the rarer action is
> In virtue than in vengeance; they being penitent,

> The sole drift of my purpose doth extend
> Not a frown further.

5, 1, 25-30

It is Prospero who does nothing but in the care of his daughter, who watches over the love between her and Ferdinand, who has to be tested by being submitted to the apparently degrading task, previously allotted to Caliban, of wood-gathering. This, to Ferdinand, is a baseness nobly undergone because it points to a rich end—a woman who quickens what's dead, in herself perfect and peerless. Once his heart has flown into her service, he promises to love, prize and honour her beyond all else in the world.

Prospero sees this right relationship as a fair encounter of two most rare affections, on which the heavens must rain grace, as they do in the fertility masque that celebrates the betrothal. But this betrothal represents a bond (a 'sanctimony', to use the language of *Troilus and Cressida*) which must be honoured. The ceremonious order of marriage must not be violated; as Prospero says:

> If thou dost break her virgin-knot before
> All sanctimonious ceremonies may
> With full and holy rite be minist'red,
> No sweet aspersion shall the heavens let fall
> To make this contract grow; but barren hate,
> Sour-ey'd disdain, and discord, shall bestrew
> The union of your bed with weeds so loathly
> That you shall hate it both.

4, 1, 15-22

This speech gives us the direct contrast between the two opposite poles of Shakespeare's moral vision; on the one hand, loving order (ceremonies, sweet aspersion let fall by heaven, a growing contract); and on the other, chaotic horror (hate, discord, disdain, weeds, hatred). Here love and order triumph over hatred and horror, if they make the right choice of spiritual love, self-control and temperance. So, in one voyage, a father (Alonso, once he has shown heart-sorrow and promised a clear life ensuing) finds a son he thought dead; that son, Ferdinand, finds a wife; Prospero finds his rightful realm; and all of them, says Gonzalo, have found themselves, where no man was his own.

If *The Tempest* is not Shakespeare's last play, then it ought to be, as it makes such a satisfying ending to his life's work.

KING LEAR

A good deal of ground has been covered in this chapter; now we turn to the one play which may be regarded as the central one in the whole canon. (The word 'central' does not necessarily mean it is the best of the plays, but that in it may be found the completest expression of Shakespeare's moral vision.) *King Lear* sums up Shakespeare's philosophy. In it, all that is implied in the dual vision of love and horror may be seen; and the action moves on four different yet related levels at the same time (the cosmos, the commonwealth, the family and the individual man), as well as being developed in two parallel stories: one of Lear and his daughters, the other of Gloucester and his sons.

Both Lear and Gloucester, deluded by professions of love, choose wrongly; both are overcome by a passion which blinds their judgment. Lear divides his kingdom; ever but slenderly knowing himself, he accepts as truth the glib and oily art of Goneril and Regan, who promise what they have no intention of fulfilling. He banishes Kent who honours him as king, follows him as master, and prays for him as a great patron; he banishes Cordelia who loves him according to her bond, returning duty as is right fit, loving, obeying and honouring him. When he disclaims paternal care and kingship, Lear acts like the barbarous Scythian whom he himself describes as feeding on his own progeny. The other, Gloucester, who as a blind man has to admit that he stumbled when he could see, similarly accepts the word of the false child, and rejects the true.

The result is a world where the old values are inverted. The physician is killed, and the fee bestowed on the disease; the father puts down his breeches, and gives the rod to his daughters; the cart draws the horse. The elements are unquiet; the kingdom scattered; two families disintegrated. A duke is blinded and left to smell his way about; a king inhabits a hovel on a storm-swept heath, goes insane, and plays at a court of justice where the accused are two joint-stools, and the judges are a professional fool and an outcast pretending to be mad. According to Gloucester this is a world of cooling love, failing friendship, division of brothers, mutinies, discord, treason, machinations, ruinous disorders, unnaturalness, dearth, malediction, banishment and nuptial breaches. According to Lear it is a world given over to adultery and thriving copulation—the exercise of riotous appetite. There is hell, darkness, a sulphurous pit, boiling, scalding, stench; a dog in authority is obeyed, and the human creature runs from the cur; the beadle lusts for the whore he is punishing for her lust; justice breaks its lance trying to pierce sin which is armed with gold-plate. The world is a great stage of fools; to be born into it is a matter for wailing and crying; to live in it is a matter of suffering endurance.

In a world such as this, where man's life has become as cheap as beast's, authority is wielded by the monsters to whom the offices of nature, bonds of childhood, effects of courtesy and dues of gratitude are meaningless. Goneril, Regan and Edmund are ones whose flesh and blood has grown so vile that it hates its begetters—they are the vile to whom wisdom and goodness seem vile; they are filths savouring but themselves. Edmund, believing that through invention (cunning) the base can top the legitimate, speaks for them all when he says: 'Let me, if not by birth, have lands by wit. All with me's meet that I can fashion fit'.

Yet there is more in *King Lear* than the vision of horror; in fact the horror itself is seen as something creative. As Lear's wits turn to madness, he comes to accept himself as a sinner rather than as one sinned against, for his own flesh is acknowledged to have created the daughters who have rejected him as both king and father. He begins to see that the world is full of poor naked wretches of whom previously he has taken too little care. When Regan says that to wilful men 'The injuries that they procure Must be their schoolmasters', she speaks truly. As Lear strips off his 'lendings' to become an 'unaccommodated man' he reaches a base on which he can rebuild. Later, when he is elbowed by shame at a past unkindness that stripped his daughter from his benediction, he puts on new clothes, and awakens to music, fair daylight and the sight of Cordelia. The breach in abused nature is cured.

Cordelia is clearly the central representative of the vision of love; she is in fact regarded by some critics as 'a Christ-figure'. At the beginning, after her sentence of banishment, she is an unprized, precious maid, most rich being poor, most choice forsaken, most loving when despised. When she reappears towards the end of the play she is seen to redeem nature from the curse her sisters have brought it to. She listens to the story of her father's suffering with patience and sorrow, not rage. Her smiles and tears are more beautiful than sun and rain; her tears themselves, holy water from heavenly eyes, are like pearls dropping from diamonds. Cordelia asks 'my royal lord, your majesty' for benediction, as he kneels before her asking for forgiveness:

> O my dear father! Restoration hang
> Thy medicine on my lips, and let this kiss
> Repair those violent harms that my two sisters
> Have in thy reverence made.

4, 7, 26-9

This is the play's chief moment of love, but it is not the only one. There is Kent, returning to serve a Lear who is no more than an empty pea-pod, refusing, like the Fool, to let go of the great wheel when it begins to run downhill, or to smile as the wind sits. There is Gloucester who finally inclines to Lear, helping him to find shelter and escape further punishment because he rebels against the unnatural dealing of a daughter who sticks her boarish fangs into the anointed flesh of a king. There is Edgar, who lovingly guides his blind father, and saves his life by thwarting his suicidal leap into destruction of body and soul at once. There is Albany, at the beginning subordinate to Goneril, but at the end one of those left to re-establish order (some editors give him the closing words to say).

In fact it is Albany who speaks most fully of the fate of those who deny loving kindness and right-relationship, of the monstrous horror that is a consequence of the world's alienation from the pattern divine justice has established:

> That nature which contemns it origin
> Cannot be border'd certain in itself;
> She that herself will sliver and disbranch
> From her material sap perforce must wither
> And come to deadly use.
> ....
> If that the heavens do not their visible spirits
> Send quickly down to tame these vile offences,
> It will come
> Humanity must perforce prey on itself,
> Like monsters of the deep.

4, 2, 32-50

SHAKESPEARE'S MODERNITY

One of the difficulties of reading Shakespeare derives from the fact that his work is based, naturally and inevitably, on the philosophical, social and religious ideas of his time—as Hamlet says, the purpose of acting is to show 'the very age and body of the time his form and pressure'. And a large portion of the Elizabethan World Picture must strike us today as either quaint or insanely irrelevant. Even if we believe in angels, and most of us do not, we are not very much concerned with distinguishing the various functions of the nine ranks, Seraphim, Thrones, Virtues, Princedoms and the rest. It may even be that the idea of love, harmony and contract as the means of man's achieving sovereignty over his lower self is unfamiliar and almost meaningless to us.

But when Shakespeare makes Ulysses talk about the 'universal wolf', he foreshadows the twentieth century; the vision of horror has become a reality in Auschwitz and Hiroshima, which make Iago and Edmund, Macbeth and Claudius, look like amateurs in villainy.

The fact that most of us have come no nearer to violence than reading about football supporters tearing out the insides of trains, or students rioting in Paris or Mexico, merely means that we are lucky. The eruption of violence has been a major feature of modern history, and consequently of modern art and literature. If, for example, you can look at one of the most famous paintings of this century—Picasso's *Guernica*, part of which is reproduced facing p. 73—you will see that Picasso's vision of horror is a pictorial cousin of Shakespeare's; and you will find it in the examples of modern writing with which this chapter ends.

W. B. Yeats, in one of his best-known poems, *The Second Coming*, wrote:

> Things fall apart; the centre cannot hold;
> Mere anarchy is loosed upon the world,
> The blood-dimmed tide is loosed, and everywhere
> The ceremony of innocence is drowned;
> The best lack all conviction, while the worst
> Are full of passionate intensity.

The first four lines, and particularly the fourth, could have been written by Shakespeare.

In the first volume of his autobiography, *Arrow in the Blue*, Arthur Koestler describes how, when he was about four, his parents took him to a strange doctor. This man, he was told, would look at his throat and give him some cough medicine. Koestler was strapped into a chair, half-senseless with fear, and became even more terrified when he saw that his parents, too, were frightened. His tonsils were then cut out, without anaesthetics:

> Those moments of utter loneliness, abandoned by my parents, in the clutches of a hostile and malign power, filled me with a kind of cosmic terror. It was as if I had fallen through a manhole, into a dark underground world of archaic brutality. Thenceforth I never lost my awareness of the existence of that second universe into which one might be transported, without warning, from one moment to the other.

This idea of a sudden descent into a world of lunatic brutality appears again and again in twentieth-century literature; for example, in Kafka's novel *The Trial* or his short story *Meta-*

morphosis, in Sartre's novel *La Nausée*, in the plays of those who have created what is known as 'the theatre of the absurd'. What Koestler describes is a breach of trust and kindness; his underground world of archaic horror is one that Lear would recognise as his 'wheel of fire', and one that is represented in *Macbeth* by the ingredients of the weird sisters' cauldron.

In William Golding's novel, *Lord of the Flies*, a number of boys are wrecked on a tropical island during their evacuation from an atomic war. Some of the boys try to establish an ordered life, compiling registers, lighting and maintaining rescue fires, building shelters, holding meetings with rules of procedure; others prefer the glamour and power of pig-hunting, brandishing knives, throwing stones that get bigger and bigger, losing their human selves behind painted masks, becoming obsessed by beating and blood-letting. At one crucial meeting there is this exchange between Ralph and Jack:

'The rules!' shouted Ralph, 'you're breaking the rules!'

'Who cares?'

Ralph summoned his wits.

'Because the rules are the only thing we've got!'

But Jack was shouting against him.

'Bollocks to the rules! We're strong—we hunt! If there's a beast, we'll hunt it down! We'll close in and beat and beat and beat —!'

'Good things of day begin to droop and drowse, Whiles night's black agents to their preys do rouse' runs a couplet from *Macbeth*. How many times has our own century been able to say that to itself?

READING LIST

J. F. Danby: *Shakespeare's Doctrine of Nature* (Faber PB, 1961).

R. M. Frye: *Shakespeare and Christian Doctrine* (Princeton/OUP, 1963).

H. C. Goddard: *The Meaning of Shakespeare* (Phoenix PB, 1960).

T. Spencer: *Shakespeare and the Nature of Man* (Collier-Macmillan PB, 1961).

E. M. W. Tillyard: *The Elizabethan World Picture* (Peregrine PB, 1963).

J. Vyvyan: *The Shakespearean Ethic* (Chatto, 1959).

7

Reading the Plays

To study the text of a Shakespeare play, as opposed to watching it, means that you are trying to define, illuminate, expound or evaluate the significance of thousands of black squiggles. In the jargon of modern literary criticism, you are trying to articulate a disciplined, critical response to the words on a page.

THE 'MEANING' OF A PLAY

But it is not easy to know exactly what the words mean, for they are often used ambiguously; and especially so in poetry, of which drama is only one branch. In a scientific report the words should bear only one clearly realised meaning; but in Shakespeare, as in all poetical writing, there are often several meanings present at one and the same time. For instance, some statements are obviously ironical, both in life and in literature: as when we say, 'A fine day, isn't it?' to a friend we meet in a rainstorm. And modern critics are adept at finding, in an apparently innocuous statement, an irony which stands it on its head.

It is very worrying to the reader when one play or poem can be interpreted in two quite opposed ways. The fact remains, however, that ambiguity is a subtle and telling literary device, that there are layers of meaning in literature, that 'symbolical undertones' really do exist. It is to our intellectual advantage to see these layers of meaning, to realise these undertones, to worry about the ambiguities. Education, it has been said, is a debate in our minds, and great imaginative literature, like *King Lear*, sets the debate going. When Sartre said that no one had a right to be innocent, and that it was the function of literature to destroy such a state, perhaps this is what he meant.

This leads to the fringe of a very difficult literary and philosophical problem: what exactly do we mean when we talk about the 'meaning' of *King Lear* or *Macbeth*? Is there in fact *the* single meaning, or are there x meanings for x readers? Is every reader equally entitled to his 'own' meaning? Obviously not quite, because some readers are more qualified (for example, by a lifetime's reading) to find a meaning than others. Again, what relationship should these x meanings have to what Shakespeare intended? And what did he 'intend'? Can we find this out? Did he know himself? The nearest we can get to this last problem is by learning about the ideas discussed by his contemporaries, by analysing the climate of his age, by studying (as we have done in a small way in Chapter 6) the history of ideas. It is clear that such historical study can illuminate the plays, but how far does it limit the meanings we can or should read into them? Shakespeare left no explicit statement of his philosophy, as, say, Bacon did; so we cannot even be certain that he was 'Elizabethan' in anything but chronology. We cannot forget that we are living in twentieth-century England, and, in the last resort, these plays are important for us only if they tell us something about our own historical position. In a way, we are *forced* to modernise the plays—but how far can we go? How far *should* we go?

Finally it is important to remember that Shakespeare was not what we might call—to modernise him—a party-writer, for whom the world is full of good goodies and bad baddies, all definable according to an established line. He was not writing thesis-dramas to show that all party-members, or upholders of the civil order against the attacks of monstrosity, were whiter than white. If, for example, we say that in *Antony and Cleopatra* Antony is a strumpet's fool betraying the values of a Roman world, of which he had been a triple pillar, for the sake of the soft Eastern beds where his pleasure lies, are we giving a fair account of a play which questions the values of both sides?

It seems better to remain content with these plays as questionings and explorations, rather than as statements, of values.

T. S. Eliot once wrote in an essay called *Shakespeare and the Stoicism of Seneca* (reprinted in *Selected Essays*):

> In any case, so important as that of Shakespeare, it is good that we should from time to time change our minds. . . . About anyone so great as Shakespeare, it is probable that we can never be right; and if we can never be right, it is better that we should from time to time change our way of being wrong.

A work of art can be regarded as a kind of looking-glass, offering a different reflection as different people look into it. What this means, and how all the problems we have just mentioned can be exemplified, can be seen in the hundreds of different interpretations of *Hamlet*; the passion with which these interpretations are offered and rebutted is some indication of the hold Shakespeare can have over the minds of his readers. (There are very useful summaries of *Hamlet* criticism in *Shakespeare Survey*, Vols. 9 and 18.)

HOW TO WORK ON A PLAY

In this section we offer a plan of campaign to those who want to study a Shakespeare play or plays in detail. We have tried to guide you through the maze of Shakespeare writings and have presented some abstruse philosophical and literary problems to you; now we can come down to earth. We hope to be forgiven if some of the advice we give sounds elementary; but the study of Shakespeare is both difficult and important, and experience shows that many people do not set about it in a logical way.

First, read the play as a whole in as few sittings as possible (it should take between two and three hours), and as fluently as you would read a modern novel. One good way of doing this is to read it aloud to yourself; another is to get hold of one of the uncut recordings (such as those of the Cambridge University Marlowe Society performances, issued by Argo), and listen to it with the text open before you. As you read or listen, try to visualise the action on the kind of stage we have described. Don't try to look anything up; don't worry if whole passages seem gibberish, because you will get the general drift of things, and will understand, if only vaguely, the shape of the whole play before you start exploring the details. This is important because some incidents and dialogue early in a play may be understandable only in the light of later developments (for example, the description of Macbeth in the opening scenes, or Duncan's first reaction to the castle where he is to be murdered). Remember that Shakespeare himself knew what was coming, not necessarily because he was the type of writer to plan everything in detail before he started, but because his plays are mainly versions of already-known stories; and there is always the possibility that he sometimes wrote scenes in non-chronological order, as the fancy took him. Particularly, you need to keep reminding yourself, increasingly so as you become involved in detail, that the plays are wholes, and are meant to be enjoyed. Your struggle to understand minor points is valuable only in so far as it leads to an increased understanding of the play.

Once you have the feel of the play you can start on the hard work. And there seems little point in pretending that reading Shakespeare (or any adult literature, for that matter) is not hard. You are being asked to understand material produced by one of the maturest minds of our civilisation, operating with tremendous intensity in a language whose idiom is just sufficiently removed from our own to make it treacherous. Ideally, in the first place you should know what all the words of a play mean in the dictionary sense; this means you should be able to explain or paraphrase in modern English any given passage. How closely you approach this ideal depends on your enthusiasm, patience and tolerance of the drudgery of looking words up every few seconds. Many think that this treatment of Shakespeare as if he were a foreign language text is the best way of making you vow never to look at the stuff again; but you cannot have any right to talk about a play until you have made this basic, strenuous effort to understand what the words mean in an elementary sense. It is not necessary to pretend that this effort is interesting, although it may be, particularly if you are linguistically inclined; it is merely achieving that familiarity with the text which is an essential preliminary to literary criticism.

Because all this looking-up is drudgery, it seems best to work at a play in the smallest meaningful units—say a scene or two at a time. If you try to do this for more than half an hour or so you get tired, and you begin to skip the hard bits. After hours of this gradual working through the play (it gets easier the more you do, as you get accustomed to Shakespearean language), it is a good idea to put all the bits together by another continuous reading of the whole. Again, this should be a useful reminder that Shakespeare did not really write plays so that examiners could ask questions about them. If you can go to see a good performance, so much the better.

Now can begin the most serious and interesting part: understanding the *significance* of what is said in addition to its *meaning*, and it is here that you will come up against the problem of differing interpretations. You probably read *The Merchant of Venice* when you were younger; we don't know what explanations you were given then, but what do you make of it when you are told that Antonio was a savage anti-semite, whose love of profit is no different from Shylock's moneylending, that Bassanio was a fortune-hunter, Gratiano a brutal Jew-baiter and Jessica a thief, that Portia exploited the court-room situation for glamorous self-aggrandisement, that Shylock, like Othello, was a noble man warped by others' villainy? At one time or another, all these views have been advanced by well-known critics. If you reply that this is not how the play appears to you, certain critics will seize upon your use of the word 'appears'; they will point out that the difference between 'appearance' and 'reality' is a favourite theme with Shakespeare, that this is the point of everything—as it is symbolised in the casket scene. In passing, to take up a point made earlier, should we know about Elizabethan attitudes to Jews and usury; do we need to have read Marlowe's *The Jew of Malta*; do we need to know about the execution in London of the Portuguese Jew, Lopez, in 1594; can we forget our knowledge of anti-semitism in our own time?

There are difficulties like this in play after play. Are Hamlet and Othello saved or damned at the end? How do we interpret Lear's last speech? Its dictionary meaning is straightforward but what about its dramatic significance? A. C. Bradley, in *Shakespearean Tragedy*, argued that Lear died joyfully, thinking that Cordelia was alive, but does this mean (a point not taken by Bradley) that Lear is back where he started, in a world of delusion? More recently it has been suggested that Lear dies knowing Cordelia is dead but unwilling to admit it—that his death, far from being a joyful one, is the play's final statement of despair, suggesting that even after repentance and the coming of self-knowledge there is nothing to prevent the repercussions of the evils released when kindness is destroyed.

What you have to do in this kind of work is what the French call *explication*; what you have to ask yourself is not 'What is Shakespeare saying here?' but 'Why is he saying this at this particular moment in the play, and what particular contribution does this make to the total impact of the presentation?' The answer to this is commentary, not paraphrase. It is hard to show you how to do this as systematically as the linguistic work, because understanding in this sense tends to be the result of a process of accumulation as you read and re-read the play, and as you discuss it with others. Here are some main headings that you can profitably consider:

1. The theme of the play

The sooner you can satisfy yourself about this, the better, for it is this which focuses everything else. The theme is not the same thing as 'what the play is about', or the sum of individual incidents. It is something more general and abstract, and the lines on which you might be thinking we tried to suggest in Chapter 6. The more plays you know, the more advantageously you will be placed; and it is most helpful to see the plays grouped as we suggest in the Bibliography, p. 156.

2. The structure of the play

What pattern does the whole action (or actions) fall into; how are individual scenes related; which advance the action, and which hold it steady? The act-divisions will not necessarily help here, and may be a hindrance by imposing on a play a five-part structure not intended by Shakespeare (although here again is material [see p. 59] for learned controversy). The way scenes are related is important because this is one of the ways a dramatist can manipulate your attitude to what is happening; an obvious example is the use of the Porter scene in *Macbeth* to point the hellish nature of what has happened in the previous scene; it has nothing to do with the 'story').

Each play has its own structure, but critics have tried to establish some basic patterns. Plays generally fall into three sections: an *exposition*, establishing the basic, potentially explosive situation, and the main character-relationships; a *development*, carrying the conflict inherent in the opening to its climax; a *dénouement* resolving this conflict, and re-establishing some form of equilibrium. It will be seen how aptly this basic pattern reflects the disruption and re-achieving of order we discussed in Chapter 6.

Attempts have been made to classify different forms of plot within this three-part structure. Some of these are:

(a) *single, episodic action:*

One action, usually centred on the fortunes of one man, proceeds by clear stages. In *Macbeth* there are three main episodes dealing with the protagonist's relationship with Duncan, Banquo and Macduff in turn; then the episode of Macbeth's defeat. The turning point of the action, after the murder of Macduff's family, is emphasised by the change of scene to England, and the dramatically static kingship-discussion (4, 3). There is a similar place change in *Othello* to separate Othello's marriage from Iago's destruction of it; the three sections of *The Winter's Tale* are marked by place changes, one of them, after a short bridge scene (3, 3), emphasised by the time-gap.

(b) *'river' action:*

Several actions, not closely connected, are kept moving in parallel, to be integrated at the end of the play. This is a favourite device in comedy, where much of the pleasure lies in the beauty of the action's pattern. *A Midsummer Night's Dream* has four threads, three of them concerned with marriage, one of these (Demetrius-Helena-Hermia-Lysander) with its own complications, and each of the four is related to the other three. *Much Ado About Nothing* and *Twelfth Night* have each three actions. But this kind of pattern is not solely comic. Both *Henry the Fourth* and *The Tempest* have three plots, each used to illustrate the other two.

(*c*) '*mirror*' *action:*

This is a simplified form of (b). Here there is a main plot and a sub-plot which is used for variety and comment. The clearest example is *King Lear*; another is *Henry the Fifth*: notice how the Chorus to the second act—'Now all the youth of England are on fire'—is followed by the petty squabbling of Nym and Pistol, and how Henry V's great 'Once more unto the breach' exhortation is juxtaposed with Bardolph's opening words in the following scene, 'On, on, to the breach, to the breach!' (3, 2).

We have dealt with structure at some length because it is a problem not often discussed by modern critics; because the way a play is put together is part of its 'meaning'; and because Shakespeare's plays can at first, with their multiplicity of events, be rather confusing. Instead of a simple, linear progression from incident to incident, there is a clustering of scenes about a central theme. This means that a scene does not always grow out of the immediately preceding one, but is related to it only in terms of the whole play. It was a failure to understand this that led Dr. Johnson to write that the events of *Antony and Cleopatra* were produced without any art of connection or care of disposition'. He did not understand Shakespeare's method of contrasting one scene with another.

3. *The characters of the play*

By this we do not mean conventional 'character sketches'. The *dramatis personae* must have some sort of individuality (they are given proper names rather than allegorical ones as in the Morality plays); had they not, Shakespeare would not be writing plays as we understand the term but some sort of debate among abstractions or symbols. Yet seeing the plays primarily as great galleries of characters has its dangers, and modern criticism has moved away from this approach (see the next section). It seems wiser to regard the characters as vehicles used to carry certain ideas or themes; to ask, not the question: 'What is the character of so-and-so?' but the question: 'What is the significance of so-and-so?' It is at least arguable that when Shakespeare becomes too interested in the personality of a character for its own sake he gets into difficulties. For example, Falstaff is given so much vitality that we are puzzled by his rejection; had Malvolio been more fully or sympathetically developed there would be a tragic note in his downfall, out of keeping with the tone of the rest of the play.

To expect Shakespeare's characterisation to have the gradualness, solidity or even consistency of that of, say, a nineteenth-century novel is to be disappointed. Thus, in *The Winter's Tale*, Leontes is largely a means of introducing disruptive jealousy and then penitence into the plot; it seems less important to worry about just when he begins to be jealous, although an actor will have to decide this; it seems futile to worry about what may have happened, before the play started, which could have caused Leontes' distrust. In the same way, Lear's decision to divide the kingdom is merely a convenient starting point for the disintegration that Shakespeare is really concerned with; to worry too much about the psychological cause of the action is to divert attention from where it should really be working— on the effects.

Remember that characters make sense only as part of a larger whole, only as they illuminate the theme—and this they do by relationship with the other characters. A useful way of assessing character, however, particularly when you already know a play fairly well, is to work through it from the angle of each of the main characters in turn. Thus, with *Antony and Cleopatra*, you would read through and analyse as you went the individual part of Antony, then Cleopatra, then Octavius and then Enobarbus.

4. The language of the play

Why does Shakespeare write any given scene as he does: in prose or verse; if in verse, of what kind? What variety of language is used; what is the blank verse like? What metaphors or imagery are being used (this is particularly important because it is one of Shakespeare's main ways—perhaps unconsciously— of showing you what is going on)? You will find these points discussed at greater length in Chapters 4 and 5.

Finally, let us refer you to an example of a close analysis of a scene, which might help your own work by setting an ideal to aim at. In D. Traversi's *Shakespeare, the Last Phase* there is an analysis of the pastoral scene in *The Winter's Tale* (4, 4), where a scene of 800 lines is given over 20 pages of detailed commentary. You will not agree with it all, but you will see perhaps how a 'disciplined, critical response' can be made.

PLAYS AND CRITICS

How much criticism of Shakespeare should you read?

It is a mistake to read any at all until you know the play pretty thoroughly, and have considered it on the lines we have just suggested. But good criticism is a great help, once you realise that your own response to the play is the paramount consideration, provided it is based on serious study and honest work. And if your time is limited, better to read the play than books about the play.

The inexperienced reader may well be bewildered by the sheer bulk of Shakespeariana. Here is an attempt to guide you through it.

First, you need not pay much attention to critics far removed in time. They are interesting to read if you want to find out the standards of taste during the periods when they were writing; and some of them, particularly Johnson and Coleridge, can be very valuable. But leave them until you know much more about the subject.

The criticism you read will be almost entirely twentieth century (see Bibliography), and it may be worthwhile to mention some of the developments in recent work on Shakespeare. Much of this work in the past, particularly during the nineteenth century, was concerned with character-analysis, with seeing the plays above all as psychological documents, and treating the *dramatis personae* as if they had an existence outside the text: sometimes this led to wondering whether Othello was brown or black, what Cordelia would have done in Desdemona's place or vice versa, what kind of girlhood was enjoyed by the heroines, or, most notoriously, how many children Lady Macbeth had. Since about 1930 there has been a reaction. As a result of the work of people like Spurgeon and Clemen on the imagery of the plays, and of the interpretations offered by G. Wilson Knight, we have come to see the plays as dramatic poems rather than as character-studies, to analyse them as gigantic, expanded metaphors by which Shakespeare explores a certain moral vision of life. This has been parallel to the general development of practical criticism with its emphasis on rigorous analysis of the words the poet puts down on paper, for example, in the work of I. A. Richards and William Empson. Further, because of continued research into the intellectual and dramatic traditions of Elizabethan England, we have come to see Shakespeare as one still heavily involved in the kind of symbolic and allegorical thought associated with the Middle Ages; we see how the plays may be linked with the Moralities which preceded them; for example, the second part of *Henry the Fourth* can be seen in these terms, with Hal as a princely Everyman pulled one way by the Good Angel as Lord Chief Justice, the other way by the Bad Angel or Vice as Falstaff. In its extreme form this symbolic approach leads to what has been called the 'Ritual School' where attempts are made to relate the plays, particularly the last ones, to the popular culture of folk-ritual, vegetation or fertility cults, or to what are called mythical archetypes: symbolic figures such as the sacrificial king which recur in European literature, one manifestation of which would be King Lear; readers of *The Waste Land* and *The Golden Bough* will understand this approach. Some of this interpretation is exciting, some of it is lunatic, but it all poses in extreme form the problem with which we started: how do you define 'meaning'; how do you know when to stop reading things into the plays; how important are the writer's intentions, and how do you define them? (See R. Hapgood's *Shakespeare and the Ritualists* in *Shakespeare Survey*, Vol. 15).

It has been said that the best commentary on any play by Shakespeare is another or all the other plays in the canon, and you will probably find that the more you know of many plays, the more each individual one will mean. You will be able to make cross-references to parallel incidents, characters or even phrases, to have the odd experience, after reading *Macbeth*, of finding in a play so far removed as *Love's Labour's Lost* the line: 'Fair in all hail is foul, as I conceive'. Obviously you cannot be expected to know closely all the plays, but it is helpful to read them in groups. Thus, if you are studying a play in great detail, you may find it useful at least to have read once or twice some of the other plays in that group. The Bibliography (page 156) has been specially arranged for this purpose. As with any grouping, you must not take the arrangement too seriously. Some of the groups make more sense than others; many of them are at least chronologically coherent. But this is largely a matter of convenience which must not imprison you. Some of the most illuminating comparisons can be made by deliberately cutting across the classification we suggest: for example, *Much Ado About Nothing*, *Othello* and *The Winter's Tale* are related by their concern with jealousy and slander; *King Lear* and *Timon of Athens* are very close; *Macbeth* and *Richard the Third* are often regarded as parallel studies of ambition and revenge, and *Macbeth* and *Julius Caesar* are studies of the faithful servant turned king-killer; *Romeo and Juliet*, *Troilus and Cressida* and *Antony and Cleopatra* all deal with the conflicts of love in a hostile society.

8

Tail Piece

You must not think that this book gives the final answer to any of the problems of Shakespeare study. It has given you some firm facts, some likely conjectures, and, we hope, some fruitful lines of thought and some useful hints for methods of study.

Even the greatest scholar and the most perceptive critic are bound by the conventional ways of thought of their own time and social circle—just as, indeed, Shakespeare himself was. Each succeeding age has seen in the plays of this universal genius a new reflection of itself and a fresh comment on its problems. To each generation its own Shakespeare.

In the polite, sophisticated world of the eighteenth century Shakespeare was regarded as a wild, extravagant genius, whose works were in need of refinement to bring them into line with contemporary modes of feeling. Emendations were directed to the laudable end of pruning the disorder of his exuberance. Nahum Tate in 1681 revised *King Lear*, giving it a love interest (Edgar and Cordelia) and a happy ending:

EDGAR: Our drooping Country now erects her Head,
           Peace spreads her balmy wings, and Plenty blooms.
           Divine Cordelia, all the Gods can Witness
           How much thy Love to Empire I prefer!
           Thy bright Example shall convince the World
           (Whatever Storms of Fortune are decreed)
           That Truth and Virtue shall at last succeed.

This version was the one invariably acted for a hundred and sixty years, and by such great players as Kean, Garrick and Kemble; critics generally made no bones about accepting it.

Indeed, as late as 1784 we read in Davies' *Dramatic Miscellanies*:

> Who could possibly think of depriving an audience, almost
> exhausted with the feelings of so many terrible Scenes, of the
> inexpressible delight which they enjoyed, when the old king in
> rapture cried out: 'Old Lear shall be a King again?'

If the lovers of the theatre could prefer this sort of stuff for
a century and a half, how can we be sure that we ourselves know
the proper way to look at Shakespeare? In the nineteenth century,
for instance, the virtuous Thomas Bowdler published his *Family
Shakespeare*, purged of all indecency and profanity—or so he
thought; but the joke is that he did not himself understand all
the indecent references, with the result that some very rude ones
were left in and are still to be met with in many editions.
Yet even today Bowdler's view of Shakespeare prevails in many
quarters. Such an attitude gives us the sentimental, Elgarian
view of Falstaff, and the super-romantic view of Hamlet, the
melancholy Dane.

In the era of fascist Europe, the 1920's and 1930's, *Julius
Caesar* was produced in modern dress, with Blackshirt uniforms
and Nazi salutes. The play was seen as a commentary on Hitler
and Mussolini and the crushing of democracy under the jack-
boot.

And now, in our own time, the latest, wildly successful and
moving production of *King Lear* shows the King and the Fool
as two nondescript tramps, like Estragon and Vladimir in
Waiting for Godot, lost in a sort of existentialist limbo. Our
despair of human progress is echoed in our welcoming of this
version as a true interpretation of Shakespeare's intentions.

As the director, Peter Brook, wrote in the *Observer* after this
production's tour in Eastern Europe:

> In countries which have known constant revolutions and *coups
> d'état*, the violence of *King Lear* had a more immediate meaning.
> In Budapest, when Lear comes on in the last scene . . . carrying
> Cordelia dead in his arms, with no other form of expression
> but that great howl, that you hear from the wings, I felt the
> audience was moved by something much more considerable

than the sentimental image of a poor old father howling. Lear was suddenly the figure of old Europe, tired, and feeling, as almost every country in Europe does, that after the events of the last 50 years people have borne enough.

It is a tribute to Shakespeare's perennial vitality that such extremes can succeed each other. The lesson for us is that we must accept all honest critical appraisals with gratitude—for they can illuminate our ignorance and stimulate our perceptions —but with reservations. Dr. Johnson, Coleridge, Hazlitt, Bradley, Granville Barker, Caroline Spurgeon, Wilson Knight, D. Traversi—these all have good advice to give us. But it is perhaps necessary to remember that the best advice of all is that of his first known editors, Heminge and Condell, in 1623:

> Reade him, therefore; and againe, and againe: And if then you doe not like him, surely you are in some manifest danger, not to vnderstand him.

Bibliography

This bibliography is arranged to show convenient groupings of the plays. Most of the books suggested here for further reading will have at least one chapter on each play in its group, and some of them are commentaries on a single play.

GENERAL

F. E. Halliday: *A Shakespeare Companion* (Penguin PB, 1964). (This is not literary criticism, but a dictionary of everything factual relating to Shakespeare. It is invaluable.)

B. Dobrée (ed): *Shakespeare, The Writer and His Work* (Longman, 1964) includes:

D. Traversi: *The Early Comedies.*

L. C. Knight: *The Histories.*

C. Leech: *The Chronicles.*

P. Ure: *The Problem Plays.*

K. Muir: *The Great Tragedies.*

F. Kermode: *The Final Plays.*

H. Fluchère: *Shakespeare* (Longmans PB, 1961).

B. Ford (ed.): *The Age of Shakespeare* (Pelican PB, 1955). (Contains a lengthy bibliography for Shakespeare and for the period.)

M. M. Reese: *Shakespeare* (Arnold, 1953).

D. Traversi: An Approach to Shakespeare (Hollis and Carter, 1968).

Macmillan's 'Casebook' Series (PB, 1968) reprints material on individual plays.

Each volume in the *New Cambridge* and the *New Arden* series (some of which are now PB) contains a critical introduction.

I. THE COMEDIES
(a) Early (1592-7)

The Comedy of Errors	*The Two Gentlemen of Verona*
The Taming of the Shrew	*Love's Labour's Lost*

(b) Late (1598-1600)

A Midsummer Night's Dream	*The Merchant of Venice*
Much Ado about Nothing	*Twelfth Night*
As You Like It	*The Merry Wives of Windsor*

C. L. Barber: *Shakespeare's Festive Comedy* (Meridian PB, 1963).
J. R. Brown: *Shakespeare and his Comedies* (Methuen PB, 1968).
H. B. Charlton: *Shakespearean Comedy* (Methuen PB, 1966).
B. I. Evans: *Shakespeare's Comedies* (OU PPB, 1967).
L. Lerner (ed): *Shakespeare's Comedies* (Penguin, 1967).
E. C. Pettet: *Shakespeare and the Romance Tradition* (Staples, 1949).
Shakespeare Survey, Vol. 8, is mainly on the comedies.

2. THE HISTORIES

(a) The first tetralogy (1590-3)

1 Henry the Sixth	*3 Henry the Sixth*
2 Henry the Sixth	*Richard the Third*

(b) The second tetralogy (1595-9)

Richard the Second	*2 Henry the Fourth*
1 Henry the Fourth	*Henry the Fifth*

(c) Miscellaneous

King John	*Henry the Eighth*

L. B. Campbell: *Shakespeare's Histories* (Methuen PB, 1964).
M. M. Reese: *The Cease of Majesty* (Arnold, 1961).
E. M. W. Tillyard: *Shakespeare's History Plays* (Peregrine PB, 1962).
J. D. Wilson: *The Fortunes of Falstaff* (Cambridge PB, 1964).
Shakespeare Survey, Vol. 6, is mainly on the histories.

3. THE ROMAN PLAYS (1600-7)

Julius Caesar	*Coriolanus*
Antony and Cleopatra	

(This grouping is more convenient than logical; it sometimes includes *Titus Andronicus*, and the last two plays could equally go with the tragedies.)

H. Granville Barker: *Prefaces to Shakespeare* 1st, 2nd and 5th series (Batsford PB, 1963).
G. W. Knight: *The Imperial Theme* (Methuen PB, 1965).
D. Traversi: *The Roman Plays* (Hollis and Carter, 1963).
Shakespeare Survey, Vol. 10, is mainly on these plays.

4. THE PROBLEM PLAYS (1602-3)

Troilus and Cressida   *Measure for Measure*
All's Well that Ends Well

(This is another unsatisfactory grouping; some critics include *Hamlet* and *Timon of Athens*.)

E. M. W. Tillyard: *Shakespeare's Problem Plays* (Chatto, 1950).

5. THE TRAGEDIES:

(a) Minor (1593-7)
Titus Andronicus   *Romeo and Juliet*
(b) Major (1601-6)
Hamlet   *Macbeth*
Othello   *King Lear*

A. C. Bradley: *Shakespearean Tragedy* (1905, Macmillan PB, 1957).
R. A. Fraser: *Shakespeare's Poetics* (Routledge, 1962).
J. Holloway: *The Story of the Night* (Routledge, 1964).
G. W. Knight: *The Wheel of Fire* (Methuen, PB, 1960).
L. Lerner (ed): *Shakespeare's Tragedies* (Pelican PB, 1963).
I. Ribner: *Patterns in Shakespearean Tragedy* (Methuen, 1960).
Shakespeare Survey, Vol. 9, is mainly on *Hamlet*, as is Vol. 5 of *Stratford-upon-Avon Studies* (Arnold, 1963); *Shakespeare Survey*, Vol. 13, is mainly on *King Lear*. All list recent criticism.

6. THE ROMANCES (1607-11)

Pericles   *The Winter's Tale*
Cymbeline   *The Tempest*

These plays, more than any of the others, gain by being read together; they make a compact group not only in their themes but in their special dramatic characteristics.

S. L. Bethel: *The Winter's Tale: A Study* (Staples, 1947).
G. W. Knight: *The Shakespearean Tempest* (Methuen, 1932); *The Crown of Life* (Methuen PB, 1965).
D. Traversi: *Shakespeare: The Last Phase* (Hollis & Carter, 1954).
Shakespeare Survey, Vol. 11, deals with the last plays.

HISTORICAL CRITICISM

For the views of older critics, two sources are convenient:

F. E. Halliday: *Shakespeare and his Critics* (Duckworth, 1958).
Anne Ridler: *Shakespeare Criticism*, 3 vols. (Oxford).